Author of Over 220 Books

WHAT WILL HAPPEN IF YOU DIE?

EDWARD D. ANDREWS

WHAT WILL HAPPEN If YOU DIE?

Should You Be Afraid of Death or of People Who Have Died?

Edward D. Andrews

Christian Publishing House

Cambridge, Ohio

Copyright © 2018 Edward D. Andrews

All rights reserved. Except for brief quotations in articles, other publications, book reviews, and blogs, no part of this book may be reproduced in any manner without prior written permission from the publishers. For information, write,

support@christianpublishers.org

WHAT WILL HAPPEN If YOU DIE: Should You Be Afraid of Death or of People Who Have Died? by Edward D. Andrews

ISBN-10: 1945757833

ISBN-13: 978-1945757839

Table of Contents

Book Description 12

Preface 14

Introduction... 16

SECTION 1 When Your Loved Ones Dies 18

CHAPTER 1 Is There Hope Beyond the Grave? A Biblical Response to the Anguish of Losing Loved Ones 19

    The Reality of Death and Grief... 19

    Biblical Insights into Death.. 20

    The Hope of Resurrection 20

    Addressing Common Questions about Death and Resurrection... 21

CHAPTER 2 Is It Normal to Feel This Way? Understanding Grief in Light of Scripture 23

    The Universal Nature of Grief.. 23

    The Righteousness of Weeping 24

    The Complexity of Grief Reactions..................................... 24

    Grieving as a Process 25

    Biblical Counsel on Grieving... 25

CHAPTER 3 How Can I Live with My Grief? A Biblical Guide to Navigating Loss 27

    Understanding Grief and Its Expression 27

    Embracing and Expressing Grief... 28

    Coping Mechanisms for Grieving.. 28

    Navigating Feelings of Guilt and Anger 29

    Seeking Comfort and Support... 29

    Applying Biblical Principles in Grief.................................. 30

CHAPTER 4 How Can Others Help? Biblical Insights on Supporting Those in Grief 31

    The Art of Listening 31

    Providing Reassurance 32

    Being Present and Available 32

    Taking Initiative 33

    Offering Hospitality 33

    Patience and Understanding 33

    The Power of Written Words 34

    The Role of Prayer 34

    What to Avoid 34

CHAPTER 5 A Sure Hope for the Dead: What Does the Bible Really Teach? 35

    The Nature of Death According to the Bible 35

    The Promise of Resurrection 36

    The Power and Willingness to Fulfill the Promise 36

    Implications of the Resurrection Hope 37

SECTION 2 What Happens to Us When We Die? 38

CHAPTER 6 Is There Life After Death? A Biblical Examination 39

    The Prevalence of Belief in an Immortal Soul 39

    The Biblical Stance on the Soul 40

    The Origin of the Immortal Soul Doctrine 40

    The Hope of Resurrection 41

CHAPTER 7 Immortality of the Soul—The Birth of the Doctrine: How Did It Begin? 42

    The Ancient Greeks and the Immortality of the Soul 42

    The Influence of Eastern and Egyptian Beliefs 43

The Babylonian Connection 43

The Historical Spread of the Doctrine 44

Contrast with Biblical Teachings 44

CHAPTER 8 The Idea Enters Eastern Religions: How Did the Concept of Immortality Permeate Eastern Thought? 46

Hinduism and the Doctrine of Reincarnation 46

Buddhism's Interpretation of Existence 47

Shinto and Ancestral Spirits 47

Taoism's Quest for Eternal Life 48

Confucianism and Ancestor Worship 48

Jainism and the Eternal Soul 48

Sikhism's Syncretic Beliefs 48

CHAPTER 9 How Did the Doctrine of Immortality Enter Judaism, Christianity, and Islam? 50

Judaism and the Influence of Greek Philosophy 50

Christianity's Adoption of Platonic Thoughts 51

The Emergence of the Doctrine in Islam 52

CHAPTER 10 In Search of Truth: Where Do We Find Answers About Life After Death? 54

The Limitations of Science and Philosophy 54

The Bible as a Unique Source 55

CHAPTER 11 Understanding the Soul: What Does the Bible Really Teach? 57

The Hebrew and Greek Perspectives 57

CHAPTER 12 Understanding Mortality: Why Do We Die According to the Bible? 60

The Biblical Narrative of Human Origins 60

The Fall Into Sin 61

Theological Implications 61

Death - A State of Non-Existence 62

CHAPTER 13 Does the Soul Survive After Death? Exploring the Biblical Viewpoint 63

Understanding the Biblical Concept of the Soul 63

What is the Spirit? 65

CHAPTER 14 Is Reunion with Our Deceased Loved Ones a Reality According to the Bible? 66

The Biblical Account of Lazarus: A Case Study 66

Understanding the Term "Resurrection" 67

The Incompatibility with the Doctrine of Immortality of the Soul 67

Who Will Be Resurrected? 68

The Resurrection: Heavenly and Earthly Hopes 68

Resurrection in Practice: Biblical Examples 69

CHAPTER 15 Why Does Understanding the Bible's View of the Soul Profoundly Impact Our Lives? 70

Freedom from Fear of the Dead 72

CHAPTER 16 1 Corinthians 15:54; John 3:16 Is there a difference between immortality and eternal life? If so, what is it? 74

CHAPTER 17 What Does the Bible Really Say About the Resurrection? 77

Resurrection is a Foundational Doctrine 78

Heavenly Hope 81

The New Earth: The Earthly Hope 83

CHAPTER 18 Does the Concept of Hell Align with Biblical Teachings of Justice and Love? 85

Understanding Sheol, Hades, and Gehenna 85

Biblical Depictions of Final Judgment 86

The Character of God and the Concept of Hell 86

The Parable of the Rich Man and Lazarus 87

Reexamining Hell in Light of Scripture 87

CHAPTER 19 What Has Happened to Hellfire: Revisiting the Doctrine Through a Biblical Lens 88

Scriptural Foundations of Hell 88

Historical Evolution of the Concept of Hell 88

Biblical Analysis of Hellfire 89

Theological Implications 89

CHAPTER 20 What Really Is Hell? Reevaluating the Doctrine in Light of Scripture 91

The Nature of Death According to the Bible 91

Understanding the Biblical Concept of the Soul 91

Hell in Biblical Language 92

The Symbolism of Fire in Biblical Teachings 92

Resurrection and Hell 92

CHAPTER 21 Hellfire—Flaring or Fading? A Historical and Theological Inquiry 94

Historical Perspective on the Doctrine of Hell 94

Biblical Foundations of Hell 94

Theological and Philosophical Considerations 95

Impact on Christian Life and Thought 95

CHAPTER 22 Eternal Torment—Why a Disturbing Doctrine? An In-Depth Examination 97

The Historical Development of the Doctrine of Eternal Torment 97

Scriptural Analysis of Hell and Eternal Punishment 98

Moral and Theological Challenges 98

Alternative Theological Views 98

Evaluating Biblical Fidelity and Doctrine 99

CHAPTER 23 Hell—Eternal Torture or Common Grave? Reexamining the Doctrine in Light of Scripture 100

Historical Perspectives on Hell... 100

The Biblical Language of Destruction.................................. 100

Interpreting the Imagery of Fire... 101

Theological Implications of Annihilationism..................... 101

Reconciling Hell with God's Justice 101

Examining Key Theological Concepts.................................. 102

CHAPTER 24 What Did Jesus Teach About Hell? Analyzing Scriptural References and Interpretations 103

Jesus' References to Hell in the Gospels 103

Interpretation of Eternal Fire and Punishment 104

Jesus' Teachings in Context 104

Jesus' Emphasis on Resurrection and Life 104

Theological Implications of Jesus' Teachings on Hell...... 105

CHAPTER 25 The Rich Man and Lazarus: What is the Underlying Message in Jesus' Parable? 106

Contextual Background of the Parable 106

Symbolic Representation in the Parable............................. 106

Interpretation of Key Elements 107

The Parable's Teachings on Afterlife and Resurrection ... 107

Theological Implications 108

CHAPTER 26 Did God Mislead Humanity in Eden? Unpacking the True Consequences of Sin......................... 109

God's Warning in Genesis: The Immediate Consequences 109

The Serpent's Contradiction and the Nature of Deception 109

The Consistency of Scriptural Teachings on Sin and Death 110

Reevaluating the Doctrine of Eternal Torment 110

Theological Implications and Modern Understanding 111

Bibliography **112**

Book Description

"WHAT WILL HAPPEN IF YOU DIE" is a comprehensive, scholarly exploration of one of life's most profound questions. This deeply researched book delves into the Biblical perspective on death, the afterlife, and the soul, offering readers a clear, scriptural understanding of what awaits us beyond the grave.

Structured into twenty-seven insightful chapters, the book begins by addressing the universal experience of grief and loss, providing comfort and hope through the lens of Scripture. It then transitions into a thorough examination of Biblical teachings on the nature of the soul, the reality of death, and the promise of resurrection. The book confronts and challenges popular doctrines such as the immortality of the soul and eternal torment, scrutinizing these beliefs against the backdrop of Biblical texts and historical context.

Key features of the book include:

- An in-depth analysis of the parable of the Rich Man and Lazarus, exploring its symbolic meanings and theological implications.

- A critical look at traditional teachings on hell, with chapters dedicated to understanding Biblical terms like Sheol, Hades, and Gehenna, and their real meanings.

- A thoughtful examination of the Biblical narrative of human origins, the fall into sin, and the consequences of disobedience as outlined in the Genesis account.

- An exploration of the contrast between the concepts of immortality and eternal life as presented in the Scriptures.

"WHAT WILL HAPPEN IF YOU DIE" is not just a theological treatise but a source of comfort and hope. It reassures believers about God's justice and love and offers a Biblically grounded perspective on the end of life, the afterlife, and the fate of the soul. This book is an invaluable resource for anyone seeking to understand death and what comes after from a Biblical viewpoint, making it essential reading for theologians, ministers, Bible students, and anyone grappling with questions about life, death, and eternity.

Preface

In this book, "WHAT WILL HAPPEN IF YOU DIE," we embark on a profound journey to explore one of humanity's most enduring and significant questions. This exploration is not just academic; it is deeply personal and spiritual. Throughout history, the shadow of death has cast a profound mystery over human existence, prompting questions that touch the core of our being: What does death mean? What lies beyond its inevitable reach?

This work is born out of a deep desire to provide answers that are not just comforting but also rooted in the solid ground of Biblical scripture. It is an endeavor to offer clarity where there is confusion, hope where there is despair, and truth where myths and misconceptions have long prevailed. Our exploration is guided by a rigorous examination of Biblical texts, supported by scholarly research and exegetical analysis.

Each chapter in this book is designed to build upon the last, forming a comprehensive narrative that brings to light the Bible's teachings on death, the afterlife, and the soul. We delve into ancient texts with a fresh perspective, seeking to understand their original context and meaning. In doing so, we confront some of the most challenging and controversial doctrines of Christian theology, such as the nature of hell, the concept of the immortal soul, and the reality of resurrection.

As a scholar deeply committed to the conservative, literal interpretation of the scriptures, I have strived to present a work that is faithful to the Biblical text while being accessible to a wide range of readers. This book is for anyone who has wrestled with the fear of death, for those who have grieved and sought comfort in their sorrow, and for all who seek a deeper understanding of what the Bible really teaches about our final destiny.

It is my hope and prayer that this book will not only inform but also transform – guiding readers to a deeper faith, a firmer hope, and a more profound understanding of life, death, and the eternal promises of God.

As you turn these pages, may you find not only answers to your questions but also the peace and hope that comes from a deeper knowledge of God's word and His plans for us beyond this life.

Edward D. Andrews

Author of 220+ books, CEO and President of Christian Publishing House, and Chief Translator of the Updated American Standard Version (UASV)

Introduction

Death, a universal inevitability, has perplexed and intrigued humanity throughout the ages. It raises profound questions about existence, the soul's journey, and the mysteries of what lies beyond the veil of life. In "WHAT WILL HAPPEN IF YOU DIE," we venture into these profound mysteries through a careful and thoughtful exploration of Biblical scripture.

This book is more than a theological discourse; it's a journey that seeks to bridge the gap between the ancient Biblical world and our contemporary understanding of life and death. It is an invitation to explore the depths of scriptural teachings and to uncover the truths that have been clouded by centuries of cultural and doctrinal shifts.

The chapters within this book are crafted to guide the reader through a series of interconnected themes - beginning with the raw human experience of grief, traversing through the Biblical understanding of the soul and the afterlife, and culminating in the exploration of some of Christianity's most significant and debated doctrines.

As we navigate these topics, we will encounter a range of scriptural interpretations and theological perspectives. The aim is not to provide simple answers but to offer a rich, nuanced understanding that respects the complexity of the scriptures and the depth of God's message to humanity.

Each chapter is designed to be both informative and reflective, encouraging readers to engage with the material not just intellectually, but also spiritually and emotionally. The book aims to be a companion in your journey of faith, offering insights that resonate with your experiences and challenges, and providing a Biblical foundation for understanding life's ultimate questions.

As you delve into this book, you are invited to approach it with an open mind and heart. Whether you are a believer seeking deeper understanding, a skeptic looking for answers, or a seeker intrigued by the mysteries of life and death, this book is intended to be a valuable resource that brings clarity, comfort, and a renewed sense of hope in the face of life's most significant transition.

In essence, "WHAT WILL HAPPEN IF YOU DIE" is not just about death; it's about life, faith, and the eternal promises that frame our existence. Let this journey enrich your understanding and transform your perspective on what it means to live and die with hope and faith.

Edward D. Andrews

SECTION 1 When Your Loved Ones Dies

CHAPTER 1 Is There Hope Beyond the Grave? A Biblical Response to the Anguish of Losing Loved Ones

The heart-wrenching experiences of losing a child, a spouse, or any loved one, as described in the accounts throughout the world every day, resonate deeply with the human experience of grief and loss. The Bible offers a unique perspective on death, providing comfort and hope in the face of what the Apostle Paul called "the last enemy" (1 Corinthians 15:26). This chapter explores the biblical understanding of death and the hope it offers. The second section of the book will go much deeper into what happens when you die.

The Reality of Death and Grief

Understanding Grief as a Natural Response

The initial reaction of denial and disbelief to the news of a loved one's death is a natural part of the grieving process. The Bible acknowledges the deep pain and sorrow that accompanies such losses, as seen in the accounts of David mourning his son Absalom (2 Samuel 18:33) and Jesus weeping at the death of Lazarus (John 11:35).

The Psychological Impact of Loss

The loss of a child or spouse is not just an emotional blow; it represents the loss of future dreams, relationships, and experiences. This aligns with the doctor's observation that the death of a child is particularly tragic and traumatic.

Edward D. Andrews

Biblical Insights into Death

Death as an Enemy

The Apostle Paul's description of death as "the last enemy" (1 Corinthians 15:26) reflects a biblical perspective that views death as unnatural and contrary to God's original purpose for mankind. This contrasts sharply with views that accept death as a normal part of life.

Resurrection: The Core of Christian Hope

The Christian hope centers on the resurrection, as taught by Jesus Christ and his apostles. This hope is rooted in historical events, such as the resurrection of Jesus, witnessed by his disciples (John 21:12-14), and his miraculous raising of others, like the widow's son at Nain (Luke 7:12-16).

The Hope of Resurrection

Jesus Christ: The Firstfruits of the Resurrection

The resurrection of Jesus Christ is the cornerstone of Christian hope. As Paul states, "Christ has been raised from the dead, the firstfruits of those who have fallen asleep"[1] (1 Corinthians 15:20). This assures believers of the reality of the resurrection.

---

[1] **Asleep in death**: In the Scriptures, we find the expressions "sleep" (κοιμάω koimaō) and "fall asleep" (κοιμάω koimaō), with both referring to physical sleep and the sleep of death. (Matthew 28:13; Acts 7:60) When the context refers to death, Bible translators can use a footnote to express to "fall asleep in death." The same is true in the Hebrew (:פֶּן־אִישַׁן הַמָּוֶת pen-isān) "sleep in death" (Psa. 13:3). "David slept (שָׁכַב shakab) with his forefathers." (1 Ki 2:10) Jesus said to the disciples, "Our friend Lazarus has fallen asleep (κεκοίμηται kekoimētai), but I go to awaken him." The disciples said to him, "Lord, if he has fallen asleep (κεκοίμηται kekoimētai), he will get well." Now Jesus had spoken of his death (θάνατος thanatos), but they thought that he meant taking rest in sleep. (ὕπνος hupnos). Then Jesus told them plainly, "Lazarus has died (ἀποθνῄσκω apothnēskō) ..." (John 11:11–13) Some have

The Promise of Resurrection for All

Paul's expression of hope towards God for the resurrection of "both the righteous and the unrighteous" (Acts 24:15) extends this hope to all humanity. This is further supported by Jesus' promise that "all those in the memorial tombs will hear his voice and come out" (John 5:28-29).

Addressing Common Questions about Death and Resurrection

Is Grieving Normal?

The Bible shows that grieving is a normal and natural response to loss. It does not signify a lack of faith but is a part of the human experience.

What Happens After Death?

The Bible teaches that death is a state of non-existence, akin to sleep (Ecclesiastes 9:5, 10). This understanding offers a clear and straightforward view of death, free from fear and superstition.

---

argued that the dynamic equivalent thought-for-thought translations, for example, (Then David **died** and was buried, NLT) are conveying the idea more clearly and immediately, but is this really the case? Retaining the literal rendering, the metaphorical use of the word sleep is best because of the similarities between physical sleep and the sleep of death. Without the literal rendering, this would be lost on the reader. Retaining the literal rendering, "slept," and adding the phrase "in death" in a footnote completes the sense in the English text. **Sense**: to be asleep in death; the figurative extension of the physical sleep in the sense of being at rest and at peace; the person in the sleep of death exists in God's memory as they sleep in death; it is only temporary for those who are physically asleep, so it will be true of those who are asleep in death. The idea that death is like a deep sleep that one awakens from at some future point is made by multiple authors and Jesus Christ when talking about Lazarus.—1 Kings 2:10; Psa. 13:3; Matt 28:13; John 11:11; Acts 7:60; 1 Cor 7:39; 1 Thess. 4:13; 2 Pet 3:4.

Will We See Our Loved Ones Again?

The hope of the resurrection provides the assurance that we can see our loved ones again. This is not just a comforting thought but a promise grounded in the reliability of God's Word.

The biblical perspective on death and resurrection offers profound comfort and hope. It acknowledges the deep pain of loss while providing a solid hope for the future—a hope based on the resurrection of Jesus Christ and the promise of a future resurrection for all. This hope is not a mere coping mechanism but a real and tangible expectation based on the teachings and actions of Jesus Christ. It reassures us that death is not the end but a temporary state before a glorious reunion, under the loving provision of a compassionate Creator.

CHAPTER 2 Is It Normal to Feel This Way? Understanding Grief in Light of Scripture

Grief, a deeply personal and often complex experience, is a universal aspect of the human condition. It's a response to loss, particularly the loss of loved ones, and manifests in various ways across different cultures and individuals. This chapter explores the biblical perspective on grief, examining scriptural accounts and principles to understand how grief is a natural, human response, and how it aligns with God's view.

The Universal Nature of Grief

Cultural Perspectives on Grieving

The expression of grief varies widely across cultures. In some societies, like in parts of northern Europe and Britain, there is a tendency to restrain emotional expression. This contrasts with other cultures where open expression of emotions is more accepted. Regardless of these cultural norms, the Bible presents grief as a universal, natural response to loss.

Biblical Examples of Grief

Scriptural accounts provide numerous examples of grief. King David's intense mourning over the loss of his sons Amnon and Absalom (2 Samuel 13:28-39, 18:33) exemplifies the depth of parental grief. Similarly, Jesus Christ's weeping at Lazarus' tomb (John 11:30-38) and Mary Magdalene's tears at Jesus' sepulcher (John 20:11-16) demonstrate that grief is a natural and acceptable response to loss.

The Righteousness of Weeping

The Acceptability of Tears

The Bible does not shun the expression of grief but rather presents it as an expected human reaction to loss. Jesus' weeping in the face of Lazarus' death and David's profound sorrow reveal that it is normal and appropriate to express grief.

The Healing Power of Mourning

As seen in the case of some, who have lost their babies to Sudden Infant Death Syndrome (SIDS), mourning can be cathartic and healing. The Bible acknowledges this aspect of grief, suggesting that expressing sorrow can lead to emotional relief.

The Complexity of Grief Reactions

Diverse Emotional Responses

Grief can manifest in various emotions beyond just sadness, including anger, guilt, and numbness. The Bible recognizes this complexity. For instance, David's multifaceted reaction to his son's rebellion and death (2 Samuel 18:33) reflects the range of emotions one can experience in grief.

Dealing with Anger and Guilt

Anger and guilt are common aspects of grief. These emotions, though challenging, are a normal part of the grieving process. The Bible does not directly address these feelings in the context of grief, but its overall message of compassion and understanding provides a framework for dealing with such emotions.

Grieving as a Process

Understanding the Grieving Process

Grief is not a single event but a journey with varying stages and emotions. The Bible, through its varied narratives, shows that grief is a process that evolves over time, allowing for a range of emotional experiences.

The Role of Community in Grieving

The Bible emphasizes the importance of community support during times of grief. Proverbs 17:17 highlights the value of companionship and support from others. Sharing one's grief with compassionate individuals can be a critical aspect of the healing process.

Biblical Counsel on Grieving

Embracing Grief as Part of Human Experience

The Bible provides a framework for understanding grief as a natural, human response to loss. It encourages individuals to express their sorrow and seek support from others.

Finding Comfort in Scripture

The promises and hope offered in the Bible can be a source of comfort during grief. The resurrection hope, in particular, offers a unique perspective on death and loss, providing a hopeful outlook on the future.

Grief, with its manifold expressions, is a natural part of the human experience, as evidenced by numerous accounts in the Bible. It is a journey that involves a range of emotions, from sadness and despair to anger and guilt. The Bible encourages the expression of these emotions, acknowledging their role in the healing process. Moreover, it offers hope and comfort through its teachings, particularly the promise of the resurrection. In understanding grief through a biblical lens, individuals can find solace and strength, knowing that their emotions are valid and that there is hope beyond their sorrow.

CHAPTER 3 How Can I Live with My Grief? A Biblical Guide to Navigating Loss

Grief, a profound human experience, often leaves individuals grappling with intense emotions. It is a journey that varies from person to person, influenced by cultural backgrounds, personal beliefs, and individual coping mechanisms. This chapter explores how the Bible offers guidance and comfort to those grieving, emphasizing that it is both normal and necessary to express and process grief.

Understanding Grief and Its Expression

Cultural Influences on Grieving

Cultural backgrounds significantly influence how individuals express grief. In some cultures, showing emotions openly is discouraged, while in others, it is expected. The Bible, however, transcends cultural norms, offering a universal perspective on grief as a natural human response to loss.

Biblical Examples of Mourning

Scriptural accounts like King David mourning his sons (2 Samuel 13:28-39, 18:33) and Jesus weeping over Lazarus (John 11:30-38) demonstrate that even the most faithful servants of God openly expressed their sorrow.

Embracing and Expressing Grief

The Necessity of Grieving

Suppressing grief can lead to physical and emotional harm. The Bible, through characters like Job (Job 10:1), shows that releasing grief is essential for healing. Expressing grief through words, as Job did, is a therapeutic process encouraged by Scripture.

Speaking and Writing as Catharsis

Communication is a powerful tool in the grieving process. Talking about one's feelings, as advised in Proverbs 17:17, can provide immense relief. For those uncomfortable with speaking, writing, as David did in 2 Samuel 1:17-27, can be an equally effective way of processing grief.

Coping Mechanisms for Grieving

The Role of Tears in Grieving

The Bible acknowledges crying as a natural response to grief (Ecclesiastes 3:1, 4). Tears are not a sign of weakness but a necessary part of the healing process. Allowing oneself to cry, as seen in the reactions to Lazarus' death (John 11:33, 35), is vital for emotional recovery.

Understanding and Managing Emotions

The unpredictability of emotions during grief is normal. Patience and self-compassion are crucial during this time. It's important to remember that grieving is not a linear process, and each person experiences it differently.

Navigating Feelings of Guilt and Anger

Addressing Guilt in Grief

Guilt is a common emotion in grief, as seen in Jacob's reaction to Joseph's presumed death (Genesis 37:33-35). It's important to recognize that such feelings, while normal, are often unfounded. Rationalizing these emotions through the lens of biblical teachings can offer solace and perspective.

Dealing with Anger

Anger, another facet of grief, should be acknowledged and expressed in healthy ways. Ephesians 4:25-26 and Proverbs 14:29-30 provide guidance on managing anger without letting it lead to destructive behaviors.

Seeking Comfort and Support

The Importance of Community

The Bible emphasizes the role of a supportive community in times of grief (Proverbs 17:17). Sharing one's burden with understanding friends or a community can provide comfort and a sense of belonging.

Turning to God for Strength

Prayer is a powerful tool in dealing with grief. Psalms 55:22 and 2 Corinthians 1:3 highlight the importance of casting one's burdens on God and seeking His comfort. Prayer can bring a sense of peace and resilience in the face of loss.

Applying Biblical Principles in Grief

Learning from Scripture

The Bible offers timeless wisdom on coping with loss. Its teachings can guide individuals in understanding their grief, expressing it healthily, and finding comfort in their faith.

The Hope of Resurrection

The Christian hope of resurrection, as outlined in 1 Corinthians 15:26 and John 5:28-29, provides a unique perspective on death. This hope can be a source of great comfort, offering a future where grief and pain will be no more.

Grief, while a challenging experience, is a necessary and natural response to loss. The Bible offers profound guidance and comfort in navigating this journey. It encourages open expression of grief, understanding and managing the complex emotions involved, and seeking support from both the community and God. Through scriptural teachings and the hope it presents, individuals can find the strength to live with their grief and eventually find peace.

CHAPTER 4 How Can Others Help? Biblical Insights on Supporting Those in Grief

In times of loss, the bereaved often grapple with profound grief, and the support of others becomes invaluable. The Bible offers practical wisdom on how to effectively comfort and assist those mourning. This chapter explores the scriptural guidance on being a source of comfort and support to the bereaved, emphasizing empathy, practical assistance, and spiritual encouragement.

The Art of Listening

Embracing the Role of a Listener

James 1:19 encourages us to be "swift about hearing," highlighting the importance of active listening. Being present and attentive to a grieving person's expression of pain and memories is a profound way of sharing their burden. It's not about providing solutions but about offering a compassionate ear.

Encouraging Open Expression

Asking open-ended questions like "Would you care to talk about it?" allows the bereaved to decide how much they wish to share. It's crucial to respect their pace and choice of expression, as each person's grief journey is unique.

Providing Reassurance

Offering Comforting Words

Proverbs 16:24 speaks of "pleasant words" as "a healing to the bones." Reassuring the bereaved that their feelings are normal and sharing stories of others who have found a way through similar losses can be uplifting. However, ensure that such reassurances are truthful and sensitive to their situation.

Avoiding Platitudes

While trying to offer comfort, it's essential to steer clear of clichés and over-simplifications that may unintentionally minimize the bereaved person's pain.

Being Present and Available

The Value of Continued Support

Proverbs 17:17 describes a true friend as one who is present in times of distress. Offering support shouldn't just be in the immediate aftermath of the loss but should continue over time, acknowledging that grief doesn't have a set timeline.

Remembering Significant Dates

Marking anniversaries and other significant dates related to the deceased can be a thoughtful way to show ongoing support. These times can be particularly challenging for the bereaved, and your presence or a simple message can provide much-needed comfort.

Taking Initiative

Practical Assistance

1 Corinthians 10:24 encourages us to seek the benefit of others. Offering practical help, like running errands or fixing things around the house, can be incredibly helpful. The key is to take initiative and offer specific assistance rather than waiting to be asked.

The Impact of Thoughtful Actions

Actions often speak louder than words. Doing something practical, even without being asked, can be a significant relief to someone overwhelmed by grief.

Offering Hospitality

The Importance of Inviting

Hebrews 13:2 reminds us not to forget hospitality. Extending an invitation for a meal or fellowship can be comforting. It's often helpful to suggest a specific time rather than a vague "come anytime" offer.

Understanding Reluctance

Be patient if the bereaved person initially declines invitations. Gentle encouragement can help, but always be respectful of their wishes and readiness.

Patience and Understanding

Responding to Emotional Outbursts

Colossians 3:12-13 advises us to clothe ourselves with compassion and patience. Understand that the bereaved might display a range of emotions, including anger or guilt. Respond with empathy rather than irritation.

The Power of Written Words

Condolence Letters and Cards

A thoughtful letter or sympathy card can be a tangible expression of care. Such gestures allow the bereaved to revisit your words of comfort when they need them.

The Role of Prayer

Offering Spiritual Support

James 5:16 speaks to the power of prayer. Praying with and for the bereaved can bring spiritual comfort and help alleviate negative emotions like guilt or anger.

What to Avoid

Avoiding Common Pitfalls

It's crucial to avoid actions that may inadvertently add to the grief. These include avoiding the bereaved due to uncertainty about what to say, pressuring them to move on quickly, or making assumptions about how they should manage reminders of the deceased.

Supporting someone in grief is a delicate balance of listening, offering practical and emotional support, and being patient and understanding. The Bible provides rich guidance on how to be a source of comfort. It teaches the importance of empathy, the power of presence, the effectiveness of practical help, and the need for patience and prayer. By following these scriptural principles, we can be a significant source of comfort and strength to those navigating the painful journey of grief.

CHAPTER 5 A Sure Hope for the Dead: What Does the Bible Really Teach?

The death of a loved one often brings about an intense period of mourning and a poignant sense of loss. This chapter delves into the Bible's teachings on death and the afterlife, offering insights into the hope it provides for those who have passed away. This hope differs significantly from the common belief in an ethereal existence in heaven, presenting instead a promise of resurrection to life on a restored Earth.

The Nature of Death According to the Bible

Understanding Death Biblically

In order to comprehend the Bible's promise of hope for the dead, it is crucial to understand its portrayal of death. Ecclesiastes 9:5 states, "*For the living know that they will die, but the dead know nothing, and they have no more reward, for the memory of them is forgotten.*" This scripture underlines the Bible's view of death as a state of non-existence, likened to a deep sleep.

The Resurrection Hope

Central to the Bible's message is the hope of resurrection. This doctrine is not about an immortal soul living on but about a restoration to life. John 5:28, 29 speaks of a time when "all those in the memorial tombs will hear [Jesus'] voice and come out."

The Promise of Resurrection

Jesus Christ's Role in Resurrection

Jesus Christ's teachings and actions while on Earth provide the foundation for the resurrection hope. His assertion in John 5:21, 28, 29 demonstrates his authority and willingness to bring the dead back to life.

The Resurrection of Lazarus: A Case Study

The account of Lazarus' resurrection in John 11 is pivotal. The detailed narrative and emotional context given in this account, especially Jesus' reaction (John 11:33, 35), underscore the reality and feasibility of resurrection. The Greek words used in the original text, such as ἐμβριμάομαι (em·bri·ma'o·mai, meaning "groaned") and δακρύω (da·kry'o, meaning "to weep"), highlight the depth of Jesus' emotional response, affirming his empathy and commitment to the resurrection hope.

The Power and Willingness to Fulfill the Promise

God's Ability to Resurrect

Acknowledging God's omnipotence is key to accepting the resurrection promise. The Creator of life is undoubtedly capable of restoring it. The resurrection is thus not a mere wish but a feasible act within God's power.

Divine Desire for Resurrection

The Bible illustrates that God is not only able, but also desirous, of resurrecting the dead. Job 14:14, 15 speaks of God's yearning to bring back those who have died. This profound longing from Jehovah assures us of His commitment to the resurrection.

Implications of the Resurrection Hope

Resurrection to a Restored Earth

Contrary to popular belief in a heavenly afterlife, the Bible's resurrection hope is firmly grounded on Earth. Scriptures like Psalm 37:29 and Matthew 5:5 indicate that the Earth will be transformed into a paradise, wherein resurrected individuals will live forever in perfect health and harmony.

The Hope for Those Who Have Died

This hope extends to all who have died – offering a chance for reuniting with loved ones and living in a world free from pain, suffering, and death, as Revelation 21:1-4 depicts.

The Bible's teaching on the resurrection provides a tangible, comforting hope that transcends traditional views of the afterlife. It reassures us that death is not the end but a temporary state preceding a glorious future. This hope is rooted in the reliable promises of God and the proven power and empathy of Jesus Christ. For those mourning the loss of loved ones, this hope offers not only comfort but also a joyous expectation of reunion in a restored (renewed) Earth.

SECTION 2 What Happens to Us When We Die?

CHAPTER 6 Is There Life After Death? A Biblical Examination

We will have a little reiteration in this introductory chapter that begins section 2. The question of life after death has been a central theme in human philosophy, religion, and thought throughout history. From the funeral rites in New York City to the cremation rituals in Jamnagar, India, humanity's quest to understand what lies beyond death is a universal concern. This chapter will explore the biblical perspective on life after death, addressing the prevalent beliefs and contrasting them with scriptural teachings.

The Prevalence of Belief in an Immortal Soul

Variations Across Cultures

Beliefs about life after death vary widely across different cultures and religions. Many Christian denominations hold to the idea of heaven and hell, while Hinduism teaches reincarnation. Islam proposes a day of judgment with paradise or hellfire as the ultimate destinations. These beliefs, while diverse, commonly hinge on the notion of an immortal soul or spirit that continues living after physical death.

Influence of Traditional and Local Beliefs

Local traditions often blend with religious teachings, creating unique practices surrounding death and the afterlife. These customs, whether from African tribes, Australian Aborigines, or West African Christians, frequently revolve around the concept of a surviving soul or spirit.

The Biblical Stance on the Soul

Scriptural Definition of the Soul

The Bible presents a different view of the soul. Genesis 2:7 describes the creation of the first man, Adam, stating that he "became a living soul." The Hebrew word used here, נֶפֶשׁ (nephesh), often translated as "soul," refers to a living, breathing creature. Thus, according to the Bible, the soul is not an immortal entity but the whole person.

The State of the Dead

Ecclesiastes 9:5 states, "For the living are conscious that they will die, but as for the dead, they are conscious of nothing at all." This scripture, among others, supports the Bible's view that death is a state of non-existence, akin to a deep sleep, with no consciousness or activity.

The Origin of the Immortal Soul Doctrine

Historical Development

The belief in an immortal soul is not rooted in biblical teachings but has its origins in ancient philosophies and religions. From Plato's concept of the soul to various pagan beliefs, the idea of an immortal soul separate from the body has infiltrated and influenced many religious teachings, including mainstream Christianity.

Contrast with Biblical Teachings

The immortal soul doctrine contrasts sharply with the biblical description of the soul. The Bible does not teach that the soul is an immortal, separable part of a person. Rather, it consistently portrays the soul as the entire living being, which can die.

The Hope of Resurrection

Biblical Promise of Resurrection

The Christian hope, as presented in the Bible, is not centered on an immortal soul going to heaven or hell but on the resurrection of the dead. Jesus Christ's words in John 5:28, 29 promise a future resurrection for those in the memorial tombs.

Jesus' Demonstrations of Resurrection

The resurrection of Lazarus in John 11 is a pivotal example demonstrating both the possibility and the reality of resurrection. Jesus' deep emotional response, as evidenced by the original Greek terms ἐμβριμάομαι (embri·ma′o·mai, "groaned") and δακρύω (da·kry′o, "wept"), reflects his empathy and the genuine nature of the resurrection hope.

The Bible presents a hope that is markedly different from the common belief in an immortal soul. It teaches that the dead are unconscious, awaiting a resurrection at a future time. This resurrection hope, exemplified in the miracles of Jesus and grounded in the promises of God, offers a comforting and tangible expectation for the future. This biblical understanding provides not only a clear answer to the question of life after death but also a realistic and hopeful perspective for those grieving the loss of loved ones.

CHAPTER 7 Immortality of the Soul—The Birth of the Doctrine: How Did It Begin?

The belief in the immortality of the soul has been a pivotal element in religious thought and practice throughout human history. This chapter explores the origins and development of this doctrine, tracing its roots from ancient civilizations to its integration into contemporary religious systems. We examine how various cultures and influential thinkers contributed to shaping this belief and how it diverged from biblical teachings.

The Ancient Greeks and the Immortality of the Soul

Socrates and Plato's Philosophical Contributions

The teachings of Socrates and his student Plato were instrumental in formulating and popularizing the concept of an immortal soul. Plato's dialogues, particularly "Apology" and "Phaedo," depict Socrates' defense of the soul's immortality, significantly influencing Western thought.

Pre-Socratic Greek Beliefs

Before Socrates and Plato, other Greek philosophers, like Pythagoras and Thales, held beliefs in the soul's continuity post-death. These ideas ranged from transmigration of the soul (reincarnation) to animistic concepts where even inanimate objects possessed a soul.

The Influence of Eastern and Egyptian Beliefs

Zoroastrianism's Impact

Zoroastrianism, the predominant religion of the ancient Persian Empire, strongly emphasized the immortality of the soul and a post-mortem judgment, influencing neighboring cultures and religions.

Egyptian Beliefs and Practices

Egyptian religious practices, particularly their elaborate burial rituals and the concept of judgment in the afterlife led by Osiris, underscored their belief in an enduring soul. This is vividly depicted in ancient papyri, such as the Book of the Dead, illustrating the soul's journey and judgment.

The Babylonian Connection

The Root in Babylonian Religion

Babylonian religion, as the source of many religious concepts for surrounding cultures, also contributed to the development of the immortal soul doctrine. Although their views on afterlife varied, the common belief in an ongoing existence after death is evident in their rituals and mythologies.

The Spread from Babylon

Following the dispersion from the Tower of Babel, as recorded in Genesis, the spread of various peoples across the globe carried with them elements of Babylonian religion, including beliefs about the soul's immortality.

The Historical Spread of the Doctrine

Integration into Major World Religions

Over time, the concept of an immortal soul found its way into major world religions, including Hinduism, Buddhism, and the Abrahamic faiths. This integration often resulted in a syncretism of original religious beliefs with the imported ideas on soul immortality.

The Role of Cultural and Philosophical Influences

Cultural exchanges and philosophical developments over centuries further entrenched the doctrine of the immortal soul in religious and philosophical thought. This was often irrespective of the original teachings of these religions, including those of the Bible.

Contrast with Biblical Teachings

The Biblical Concept of the Soul

In contrast to these beliefs, the Bible presents the soul (Hebrew: נֶפֶשׁ, nephesh) as a living, breathing being, which is mortal. Key scriptures like Genesis 2:7 and Ezekiel 18:4 underscore this understanding, which stands in stark contrast to the immortal soul doctrine.

The State of the Dead in the Bible

The Bible describes death as a state of unconsciousness, as evidenced in Ecclesiastes 9:5 and John 11:11-14. This understanding is fundamentally different from the belief in an ongoing conscious existence of the soul post-death.

The doctrine of the immortality of the soul, while deeply ingrained in many religious traditions, finds its roots in ancient civilizations like Egypt, Persia, and particularly Babylon. Its spread across various cultures and its incorporation into different religious systems, including aspects of Christianity, represents a significant departure from the original biblical teachings about death and the soul. As a result, the popular understanding of life after death in many religions today reflects these ancient influences more than it does the teachings of the Bible. Understanding this historical development is crucial for anyone seeking to reconcile these widespread beliefs with the biblical narrative.

CHAPTER 8 The Idea Enters Eastern Religions: How Did the Concept of Immortality Permeate Eastern Thought?

The belief in the immortality of the soul, though not originally part of many Eastern religions, gradually became a core tenet. This chapter explores the historical and cultural pathways through which the concept of an immortal soul entered and became embedded in Hinduism, Buddhism, Jainism, Sikhism, Shinto, and Taoism. We will examine how these religious traditions, rooted in diverse philosophies and practices, came to embrace and adapt this idea.

Hinduism and the Doctrine of Reincarnation

Origins in the Indus Valley

Hinduism, one of the oldest religions originating along the Indus and Ganges rivers, initially recognized the soul as distinct from the body, but its early texts do not explicitly mention immortality. The practice of ancestor worship and offerings for the dead suggest a belief in some form of continued existence.

Influence of Greek and Eurasian Thought

The sixth century B.C.E. saw the fusion of local beliefs with the concepts of soul transmigration and Karma introduced by Eurasian tribes. This syncretism led to the development of the doctrine of reincarnation, which became central to Hindu thought.

Brahman-Ātman and the Pursuit of Liberation

The philosophical concept of Brahman-Ātman, signifying the supreme eternal soul, further influenced Hindu beliefs. The goal of escaping the cycle of rebirth to merge with Brahman shaped the Hindu view of immortality.

Buddhism's Interpretation of Existence

Buddha's Reformulation

Emerging from Hinduism, Buddhism under Siddhārtha Gautama introduced a nuanced view of existence. Buddha taught a continuous cycle of rebirth driven by Karma but refrained from affirming a permanent soul.

The Concept of Nirvana

Nirvana, the ultimate goal in Buddhism, is portrayed not as eternal bliss but as an escape from the cycle of rebirth, leading to a state of nonexistence or the cessation of individual consciousness.

Shinto and Ancestral Spirits

Early Japanese Beliefs

Before Buddhism's introduction to Japan, Shinto focused on rituals and customs, including rites to appease the spirits of the departed. This developed into ancestor worship, with rituals to purify and elevate the status of ancestral spirits.

Taoism's Quest for Eternal Life

Taoism and the Harmony with Nature

Taoism, founded by Lao-tzu, sought harmony with the Tao, the way of nature. This harmony was believed to potentially grant immunity to death, leading to efforts to discover elixirs of immortality and achieve a state beyond physical harm.

Confucianism and Ancestor Worship

Confucius and Social Morality

Although Confucius did not extensively discuss the afterlife, he upheld and emphasized ancestor worship, focusing on the observance of rites for departed ancestors, which played a significant role in Confucian thought.

Jainism and the Eternal Soul

Mahāvīra's Teachings

Founded in the same period as Buddhism, Jainism, established by Mahāvīra, posited that all living beings possess eternal souls. Liberation from the bondage of Karma and the cycle of rebirth is achievable through extreme self-discipline and nonviolence.

Sikhism's Syncretic Beliefs

Fusion of Hindu and Islamic Concepts

Sikhism, founded by Guru Nānak in the 16th century, merged elements of Hinduism and Islam. It adopted the Hindu beliefs of soul immortality, reincarnation, and Karma, forming a unique religious identity.

WHAT WILL HAPPEN If YOU DIE?

The belief in the immortality of the soul entered Eastern religions through a complex interplay of cultural exchanges, philosophical developments, and religious reforms. While these religions originally may not have embraced this concept, over time, they integrated and adapted it into their doctrines, often blending it with their core teachings and practices. This integration has profoundly influenced the religious landscape of Asia, shaping the spiritual beliefs and practices of millions. Understanding this historical development provides insight into the diverse ways the idea of an immortal soul has been perceived and interpreted across different Eastern religious traditions.

Edward D. Andrews

CHAPTER 9 How Did the Doctrine of Immortality Enter Judaism, Christianity, and Islam?

The concept of an immortal soul that lives on after death is a central tenet in many religions, including Judaism, Christianity, and Islam. This chapter examines the historical development of this idea within these faiths, tracing its origins and the influences that shaped its integration.

Judaism and the Influence of Greek Philosophy

Early Jewish Beliefs

Initially, Jewish understanding, as reflected in the Hebrew Scriptures, did not encompass the notion of an immortal soul. The belief system during the biblical period saw the soul as inseparable from the body, ceasing to exist upon death.

Hellenistic Influence

The infiltration of Greek philosophy, particularly after Alexander the Great's conquests, introduced new concepts to Jewish thought. The translation of Hebrew Scriptures into Greek (the Septuagint) further facilitated the blending of Jewish religious beliefs with Greek philosophical ideas.

The Role of Philo and Other Jewish Philosophers

Philo of Alexandria and later Jewish thinkers, influenced by Platonic philosophy, began interpreting Jewish scriptures through the lens of Greek thought, integrating the concept of an immortal soul into Jewish theology.

The Talmud and Post-Biblical Literature

The Talmud, reflecting centuries of rabbinical teachings, shows a clear belief in the continuation of the soul after death. This shift marked a significant departure from earlier scriptural teachings.

Christianity's Adoption of Platonic Thoughts

The Early Christian Church

The teachings of Jesus Christ, as recorded in the Christian Greek Scriptures, did not advocate the immortality of the soul. However, after the death of the apostles, there was a gradual departure from original Christian teachings.

Influence of Early Church Fathers

Origen and Augustine, heavily influenced by Platonic and Neoplatonic thought, integrated the immortal soul doctrine into Christian theology. This fusion of Greek philosophy with Christian doctrine marked a significant shift from the teachings of Jesus and his apostles.

The Role of Thomas Aquinas

Aquinas, influenced by Aristotelian philosophy, modified Aristotle's view on the soul to align with the church's teaching of its immortality. His synthesis of Aristotelian thought with Christian theology solidified this belief within the church.

The Impact of the Renaissance and Reformation

The Renaissance revived interest in Plato's works, reinforcing the doctrine of the immortal soul in Christian thought. The Reformation, while challenging certain church teachings, did not alter this fundamental belief.

The Emergence of the Doctrine in Islam

The Foundation of Islamic Beliefs

The Quran, Islam's holy book, teaches the continuation of the soul's existence after death. This belief was integrated into Islamic theology from its inception, differing from the earlier Hebrew and Christian texts.

Concepts of Barzakh and Judgment

In Islamic teaching, the soul enters an intermediate state (Barzakh) after death, awaiting final judgment. This belief system encompasses both the idea of an ongoing existence of the soul and a resurrection for judgment.

Influences of Pre-Islamic Beliefs and Greek Philosophy

While Islam developed independently of direct Greek influence, its foundational beliefs were shaped in a cultural milieu where Greek philosophical ideas had permeated. The Islamic understanding of the soul reflects a synthesis of pre-Islamic Arabian beliefs and the broader religious and philosophical context of the era.

The doctrine of the immortality of the soul, now a core belief in Judaism, Christianity, and Islam, originated from sources external to their earliest scriptures. In Judaism and Christianity, it emerged through the integration of Greek philosophical ideas, particularly Platonism and Neoplatonism. In Islam, while the concept was present from its beginning, it developed within a cultural context influenced by a mix of Arabian beliefs and the broader Greco-Roman philosophical heritage. Understanding how this doctrine entered these major world religions provides insight into the evolution of their theological frameworks and the divergence of contemporary religious beliefs from their scriptural origins.

CHAPTER 10 In Search of Truth: Where Do We Find Answers About Life After Death?

The quest to understand the afterlife has been a central theme in human inquiry. With the multitude of beliefs about the soul's immortality and the nature of the afterlife, one must ask: Where can we find reliable answers? This chapter explores various avenues of inquiry and their ability to provide clarity on this profound question.

The Limitations of Science and Philosophy

Scientific Exploration of Near-Death Experiences

1. **Scientific Inquiry**: Modern science, with its empirical methodology, has investigated phenomena like near-death experiences. However, these investigations offer limited insights into the nature of life after death.

2. **Inconclusive Evidence**: While intriguing, near-death experiences cannot conclusively prove the existence of an afterlife or the nature of the soul. The interpretations of these experiences are often subjective and varied.

Philosophy's Diverse Speculations

1. **Philosophical Theories**: Throughout history, philosophers have pondered the concept of the soul and the afterlife. Their conclusions, however, are as diverse as the schools of thought they represent.

2. **Speculative Nature**: Philosophy, being largely speculative, offers various interpretations but lacks empirical evidence to assert definitive conclusions about the afterlife.

The Bible as a Unique Source

Historical Accuracy and Prophetic Fulfillment

1. **Ancient Wisdom**: The Bible predates many religious texts and provides a historical account from the beginning of humanity. Its age and continuity offer a unique perspective.

2. **Prophetic Precision**: Unlike any other book, the Bible contains prophecies that have been fulfilled with remarkable accuracy, suggesting a source beyond human foresight.

The Bible's Authority

1. **Divine Inspiration**: The Bible claims to be inspired by God, the Creator of life. This gives it a unique authority on matters pertaining to life and death.

2. **Consistent Teachings**: Unlike philosophical or cultural beliefs that have evolved over time, the Bible has maintained a consistent message regarding the soul and the afterlife.

Examining the Biblical View of the Soul

The Soul in Biblical Context

1. **Definition of the Soul**: The Bible defines the soul (Hebrew: נֶפֶשׁ, nephesh; Greek: ψυχή, psyche) not as an immortal entity, but as a living being, encompassing both physical and mental aspects of life.

2. **The State of the Dead**: Scriptural texts like Ecclesiastes 9:5 and Ezekiel 18:4 present a view of death as a state of non-

existence or unconsciousness, challenging the notion of an immortal soul.

Resurrection and Hope

1. **Biblical Promise of Resurrection**: The Bible offers the hope of resurrection as a restoration to life, as seen in accounts like Lazarus' resurrection (John 11) and the future resurrection hope (John 5:28, 29).

2. **Condition of the Resurrected**: The Bible describes a future where those resurrected will live on earth in improved conditions, contrary to the idea of an ethereal afterlife.

In the search for truth about the afterlife and the nature of the soul, the Bible stands out as a unique and authoritative source. Its historical accuracy, prophetic fulfillment, and consistent teachings provide a solid foundation for understanding these profound topics. By examining the biblical perspective, one gains clarity on the nature of the soul, the state of the dead, and the hope for the future, diverging from the varied and often contradictory views presented by science, philosophy, and cultural beliefs. As we delve into the biblical narrative, we find coherent and satisfying answers to our deepest questions about life after death.

CHAPTER 11 Understanding the Soul: What Does the Bible Really Teach?

The concept of the soul has been a subject of deep contemplation and varied interpretations throughout human history. The Bible, a source revered by many for spiritual guidance, offers a distinctive perspective on what the soul is. This chapter delves into the biblical understanding of the soul, challenging common misconceptions and exploring its implications.

The Hebrew and Greek Perspectives

The Hebrew Word 'Nephesh'

1. **Biblical Definition**: In the Hebrew Scriptures, the word for 'soul' is 'nephesh'. It is used to denote a whole being, reflecting a person or an animal as a living entity.

2. **Key Examples**: Genesis 2:7 describes Adam becoming a living soul, indicating that the soul is not an independent entity within a person but the person himself. Other examples, such as Leviticus 5:1 and Job 19:2, reinforce this holistic understanding.

The Greek Word 'Psyche'

1. **New Testament Usage:** In the Christian Greek Scriptures, 'psyche' often translates as 'soul'. Like 'nephesh', it frequently represents the whole person or animal.

2. **Illustrative References**: Passages like John 12:27 and 1 Peter 3:20 use 'psyche' to describe persons in their entirety, not an immortal element within them.

'Soul' in the Context of Animals

1. **Inclusivity in Definition**: Genesis 1:20, 24 shows that the term 'soul' applies to animals as well as humans, further emphasizing the soul as a living creature, not an immortal essence.

'Soul' as Life Force

1. **Life and the Soul**: Sometimes, 'soul' refers to life itself. For instance, Leviticus 17:11 speaks of the soul as the life in the flesh, not an immortal component.
2. **Soul in Danger or Loss**: Biblical expressions about endangering or losing one's soul (Matthew 20:28; Philippians 2:30) refer to risking or giving up life.

Misconceptions About the Soul

1. **Contrasting with Greek Philosophy**: The Bible's view of the soul is distinctly different from the Greek philosophical concept of an immortal soul.
2. **Impact of Hellenistic Thought**: Over time, Hellenistic philosophy influenced religious thinking, leading to widespread belief in an immortal soul, a concept not supported by original biblical texts.

The State of the Dead

1. **Consciousness in Death**: Ecclesiastes 9:5 states that the dead are unconscious, challenging the idea of a soul that lives on after death.

2. **Resurrection, Not Immortality**: The Bible teaches resurrection as a hope for the dead (John 5:28, 29), contrasting with the concept of inherent immortality.

The Bible presents a consistent and clear understanding of the soul, significantly different from traditional religious views. It identifies the soul as the entire living being, whether human or animal, and not as an immortal entity within. This understanding has profound implications for our view of life, death, and hope beyond the grave. By returning to the original biblical languages and context, we gain a deeper and more accurate insight into one of humanity's most fundamental questions: What is the soul?

Edward D. Andrews

CHAPTER 12 Understanding Mortality: Why Do We Die According to the Bible?

The inevitability of death is a universal human experience, yet its explanation remains a subject of great theological and philosophical debate. The Bible offers a unique perspective on why death occurs, attributing it to the earliest chapters of human history. This chapter explores the biblical explanation for the existence of death and its implications for humanity.

The Biblical Narrative of Human Origins

Creation and Perfection

1. **Genesis Account**: Genesis 1:31 and 2:15 describe the creation of the first humans, Adam and Eve, in a state of perfection, placed in a paradisiacal setting called the Garden of Eden.

2. **Eternal Life as a Possibility**: Originally, humans were created with the potential for eternal life, indicated by Ecclesiastes 3:11, which speaks of God putting "eternity" or "a sense of eternity" in human hearts.

The Command and Its Conditions

1. **God's Directive**: Genesis 2:16,17 records God's command to Adam regarding the tree of the knowledge of good and bad, establishing obedience as the key to maintaining their perfect state and potential for eternal life.

The Fall Into Sin

The Act of Disobedience

1. **The Temptation and Fall**: Genesis 3:1-6 narrates the temptation by the serpent (later identified as Satan) and the subsequent disobedience of Adam and Eve.
2. **Consequences of Disobedience**: Their act of disobedience, as explained in Romans 5:12, introduced sin into the human experience, severing the possibility of eternal life for them.

Sin's Inheritance and Death as a Penalty

1. **Transmission of Sin**: The sin of Adam and Eve, being a fundamental alteration of their nature, was passed down to their offspring, as implied in Job 14:4 and Psalm 51:5.
2. **Death as Wages of Sin**: Romans 6:23 identifies death as the direct consequence or "wages" of sin, implying that mortality is not a natural condition but a result of sin.

Theological Implications

The Loss of Perfection

1. **Degradation from the Ideal State**: Adam and Eve's sin resulted in the loss of their perfect state, both physically and morally.
2. **Impact on All Humanity**: This imperfection, including susceptibility to death, has been inherited by all humanity.

The Role of Free Will and Responsibility

1. **Human Agency in the Fall**: The account highlights the role of human choice and responsibility in the fall from perfection.

2. **Divine Justice and Human Accountability**: This narrative underscores the biblical view of divine justice, where death is not arbitrary but a consequence of moral failure.

Death - A State of Non-Existence

The Nature of Death According to the Bible

1. **Death as a Return to Dust**: Genesis 3:19 describes death metaphorically as a return to dust, indicating a cessation of life.
2. **The State of the Dead**: Ecclesiastes 9:5,10 and Psalm 146:4 depict death as a state of unconsciousness, countering the notion of an immortal soul.

The biblical narrative presents death not as an inherent part of human nature but as a tragic outcome of the first humans' disobedience. This perspective provides a framework for understanding the human condition, highlighting the themes of free will, responsibility, and the hope of redemption. While science offers insights into the biological aspects of death, the Bible addresses its moral and spiritual dimensions, offering a comprehensive explanation of why we die.

WHAT WILL HAPPEN If YOU DIE?

CHAPTER 13 Does the Soul Survive After Death? Exploring the Biblical Viewpoint

The belief in an immortal soul that continues to exist after death is a cornerstone of many religious philosophies. However, the New Catholic Encyclopedia acknowledges that this concept is not easily found in the Bible. This chapter seeks to explore the biblical perspective on the nature of the soul and what happens to it at death.

Understanding the Biblical Concept of the Soul

The Soul as a Living Being

1. **Biblical Definitions**:
    - The Hebrew word "ne'phesh" and the Greek word "psy·khe'," often translated as "soul," frequently refer to a living being or the whole person.
    - Scriptural examples: Genesis 2:7 describes Adam as becoming a living soul, indicating that the soul is the person himself.

The Soul's Mortality

1. **Soul Subject to Death**:
    - The Bible clearly states: "The soul that is sinning—it itself will die." (Ezekiel 18:4)
    - This contradicts the idea of an inherently immortal soul.

The Condition of the Dead

Unconsciousness in Death

1. **Biblical Statements on Death:**
    - Ecclesiastes 9:5,10 speaks of the dead as having no consciousness or activity.
    - This is supported by Psalms and other scriptures, which describe death as a state of nonexistence or sleep.

The Soul Dies

1. **Examples of Soul Death in Scripture:**
    - References to "a deceased soul" or instances where individuals, such as Elijah and Jonah, wished for their souls to die, reinforce the concept that the soul is not immortal.

The Meaning of 'Soul Going Out' and 'Coming Back'

1. **Biblical Usage in Context:**
    - Genesis 35:18 on Rachel's death and 1 Kings 17:22 on the resurrection of the widow's son need to be understood contextually as referring to the life-force, not an immortal soul.

The Dilemma of the Intermediate State

1. **Problem of Conscious Existence Post-Death:**
    - The intermediate state, as taught in some Christian doctrines, is not supported by the Biblical concept of death as a state of unconsciousness.

What is the Spirit?

The Spirit as Life-Force

1. **Biblical Definition:**

    - The spirit (Hebrew, ru'ach; Greek, pneu'ma) in the Bible often means breath or life-force.

    - This life-force ceases at death, as described in Psalm 146:4.

The Return of the Spirit to God

1. **Ecclesiastes 12:7 Explained:**

    - The returning of the spirit to God does not imply a conscious existence but rather that the hope of future life or resurrection is in God's hands.

The Bible presents a clear and consistent picture of the soul. It is not an immortal entity that lives on after the physical death of a person. Death is described as a state of nonexistence, similar to deep sleep, with no consciousness or activity. The soul, being the person himself or the life-force within, dies and does not continue in any form of conscious existence. The resurrection hope, as promised in the Bible, is the means by which God can restore life to those who have died. This understanding not only aligns with the scriptural narrative but also offers a coherent explanation of the human condition in relation to life and death.

Edward D. Andrews

CHAPTER 14 Is Reunion with Our Deceased Loved Ones a Reality According to the Bible?

The inevitability of death is a universal truth that every human must confront. The profound sorrow and sense of loss that accompany the death of a loved one often lead to the poignant question: Is there a possibility of being reunited with them? The Bible presents a clear doctrine of resurrection, offering a sure hope for the future.

The Biblical Account of Lazarus: A Case Study

The Miraculous Resurrection of Lazarus

- In 32 C.E., Lazarus of Bethany fell seriously ill. His sisters, Martha and Mary, sent for Jesus, who was then across the Jordan River.

- Jesus, upon arriving in Bethany, found that Lazarus had been dead for four days.

- Jesus performed a remarkable miracle, bringing Lazarus back to life, demonstrating His power over death and reinforcing the faith of many in the resurrection hope.

Understanding the Term "Resurrection"

The Original Meaning

- The Greek word a·na′sta·sis, translated as "resurrection," literally means "a standing up again," indicating a return to life from death.

- In the Hebrew Scriptures, although the term "resurrection" is not directly used, the concept is present in texts like Job 14:13, Daniel 12:13, and Hosea 13:14.

Jehovah God's Role

- As the Creator and Source of life, God has the ability and the desire to resurrect the dead.

- Jesus Christ, empowered by God, demonstrated this ability through various resurrections he performed during his earthly ministry.

The Incompatibility with the Doctrine of Immortality of the Soul

Biblical Clarification

- The resurrection hope as presented in the Bible contradicts the idea of an immortal soul living on after death.

- Martha's statement about Lazarus' future resurrection, "on the last day" (John 11:24), indicates a belief in resurrection, not in an immortal soul.

Who Will Be Resurrected?

The Righteous and the Unrighteous

- Jesus Christ promised that "all those in the memorial tombs" will hear his voice and come out (John 5:28, 29).

- The Bible assures a resurrection for both the righteous and the unrighteous, providing a hope for countless individuals who have died, often without a clear understanding of God's purposes.—Acts 24:15.

The Resurrection: Heavenly and Earthly Hopes

A Limited Heavenly Resurrection

- A select group, numbering 144,000, will be resurrected to heavenly life to rule with Christ. These are chosen from among Christ's followers, starting from the first-century Christians. Robert L. Thomas, Jr., professor of New Testament at The Master's Seminary in the United States, wrote: "The case for symbolism is exegetically weak." He added: "It is a definite number [at 7:4] in contrast with the indefinite number of 7:9. If it is taken symbolically, no number in the book can be taken literally."—*Revelation: An Exegetical Commentary,* Volume 1, page 474.

- They will be given spirit bodies to exist in heaven.

A Global Earthly Resurrection

- The vast majority of resurrected ones will live on a renewed, paradisiac earth.

- This future earth will be devoid of pain, suffering, and death, fulfilling God's original purpose for mankind.—Revelation 21:4; Psalm 37:29.

Resurrection in Practice: Biblical Examples

Instances Demonstrating Resurrection

- The resurrections performed by Jesus, including that of Lazarus, the widow's son at Nain, and the daughter of Jairus, provided clear evidence of the joy and hope resurrection brings.
- These miracles prefigured the larger-scale resurrection to come in God's new world.

The Bible's teaching on resurrection offers a sure hope that transcends the despair and finality of death. This hope is not based on the immortality of the soul, but on God's promise and ability to restore life to those who have died. For millions, the resurrection will mean an opportunity to live on a renewed earth, free from suffering and death. This biblical hope provides comfort and encouragement, influencing how we view death and how we live our lives today. The resurrection hope is integral to the Christian faith, offering a profound answer to humanity's longing for life beyond death.

Edward D. Andrews

CHAPTER 15 Why Does Understanding the Bible's View of the Soul Profoundly Impact Our Lives?

The topic of the soul and its fate after death has intrigued humanity for millennia. The Bible's perspective on the soul is distinct from many traditional views and profoundly affects how we understand life, death, and hope. This chapter explores why it's essential to examine our beliefs about the soul and death and how the Bible's teachings provide comfort and hope.

A. Confidence in the Bible's Teaching About the Soul

Authenticity and Consistency of Scriptural Texts

- The Bible's manuscripts are remarkably well-preserved and consistent over centuries, lending credibility to its message.

- Scriptural prophecies that have been fulfilled add to our confidence in the Bible's reliability.

Logical and Clear Explanations

- The Bible offers a clear and logical explanation of the soul, distinct from the often ambiguous and contradictory views found in many philosophies and religions.

- Its teachings align with observable realities about life and death, avoiding the pitfalls of speculative doctrines.

B. The Biblical Truth About the Soul

The Soul as a Living Being

- The Bible defines the soul (Hebrew: ne′phesh; Greek: psy·khe′) as a living, breathing creature, not an immortal entity.
- Scriptures like Genesis 2:7 and Ezekiel 18:4 reveal that the soul is mortal and subject to death.

Implications of This Understanding

- This view of the soul aligns with the observable reality that life ceases at death.
- It eliminates the fear of an afterlife of suffering or the unknown, offering a straightforward understanding of our existence.

A. Dispelling the Fear of Death

The Bible's View as a Source of Comfort

- Understanding that the dead are in a state of non-existence, as Ecclesiastes 9:5, 10 explains, removes the fear of the dead suffering or watching over the living.
- It provides comfort to those grieving, knowing their loved ones are not enduring pain or distress.

Courage in the Face of Terminal Illness

- The resurrection hope as promised in the Bible gives courage to individuals facing terminal illness.
- Example: A terminally ill teenager finds solace in the hope of the resurrection, alleviating the fear of death and the unknown.

B. Liberation from Despair Over Death

Hope in the Resurrection

- The Bible's promise of a resurrection (John 5:28, 29; Acts 24:15) offers real hope and comfort, replacing despair with the prospect of life after death.
- This hope is grounded in historical events, like the resurrection of Lazarus, demonstrating its feasibility.

Illustration of Comfort

- A grieving family finds comfort in the resurrection hope, mitigating the pain of their loss.
- They are reassured by the scriptural promise that they can see their deceased loved ones again under peaceful conditions on earth.

Freedom from Fear of the Dead

Understanding the State of the Dead

- The Bible teaches that the dead are unconscious, which dispels superstitious fears related to the dead, such as haunting or the need for rituals to appease them.
- This understanding frees people from the psychological and emotional burdens associated with such fears.

Comfort in Mourning

- Acknowledging the Bible's teaching on the soul provides a healthier perspective in mourning, focusing on remembering and honoring the life lived rather than fearing the current state of the deceased.
- It encourages a more grounded and realistic approach to death and the grieving process.

WHAT WILL HAPPEN If YOU DIE?

Understanding the Bible's teaching about the soul has a transformative impact on how we view life, death, and our future hope. It dispels fears and superstitions, brings comfort to the grieving, and provides a firm foundation for hope in the resurrection. This biblical view frees individuals from despair and uncertainty, offering a clear and hopeful perspective on what happens after death.

Edward D. Andrews

CHAPTER 16 1 Corinthians 15:54; John 3:16 Is there a difference between immortality and eternal life? If so, what is it?

1 Corinthians 15:54 Updated American Standard Version (UASV)

54 When the perishable puts on the imperishable, and the mortal puts on **immortality**, then shall come to pass the saying that is written: "Death is swallowed up in victory."

John 3:16 Updated American Standard Version (UASV)

16 For God so loved the world that he gave his only begotten Son, in order that whoever believes in him will not be destroyed but have **eternal life**.

IMMORTALITY: (ἄφθαρτος aphthartos) immortal, imperishable, indestructible, cannot be destroyed, so, of course, it means lasting forever

ETERNAL LIFE: (ζωὴν αἰώνιον zōē aiōnion) means eternal, an unlimited duration.

This is not really semantics because, if taken literally, immortality means the being is imperishable and indestructible, which means the being cannot be destroyed. The Greek word translated "immortality" (ἀφθαρσία aphtharsia) is formed from the negative "a" and from (θάνατος thanatos), meaning "death." Therefore, the basic sense of immortality is 'without death.' It has always been that only God was indestructible (Psalm 36:9; 90:1-2). The Son, who is "the radiance of his glory and the exact representation of his nature," is described as "the blessed and only Sovereign, the King of those who reign as kings and Lord of those who rule as lords, **the one who alone possesses immortality**."

WHAT WILL HAPPEN If YOU DIE?

(Hebrews 1:3; 1 Timothy 6:15-16) No creature can take The Father or the Son's life as they are immortal, which makes them different from humans or angels, that are destructible.

Even Michael the archangel, the highest-ranking angel and the second most powerful being there, is, aside from God, destructible. That is, he can be destroyed. So, the question that now begs to be asked will everyone who receives eternal life be immortal? I highly doubt that. Those that go to heaven will receive immortality, which encompasses eternal life, and those on earth will receive eternal life. However, they can still be destroyed, which is clear from what will happen to some after the thousand-year reign of Christ when some will be tempted by Satan and receive the Second Death from which there is no resurrection. Even though *Adam and Eve were* created to live forever, they *were* not *immortal*. So, immortality does encompass the sense of eternal life, but it is beyond that as it implies more than the fact that the person having immortality will live forever. It is connected with incorruption, which is imperishable, indestructible, cannot be destroyed, and cannot die.

1 Corinthians 15:53-55 Updated American Standard Version (UASV)

53 For this perishable must put on the imperishable, and this mortal must put on **immortality**. 54 When the perishable puts on the **imperishable**, and the mortal puts on **immortality**, then shall come to pass the saying that is written:

"Death is swallowed up in victory."
55 "O death, where is your victory?
O death, where is your sting?"

However, the Bible does not offer us many insights into what life will be like for those who receive immortality. As was said above, Adam and Eve possessed eternal life. And we know that they had to eat food and drink water to maintain life. It can be inferred that if, hypothetically, they stopped eating and drinking water, they would die, and they would experience corruption, even though they possessed eternal life. (Genesis 2:9, 15, 16) There is nothing within the Scriptures that would suggest that those who will receive immortal life in heaven with spirit bodies will need to consume something to sustain their eternal life. Thus, immortals are not subject to death. When they receive their spirit body, they will be imperishable, receiving incorruptibility. (Compare 2 Corinthians 5:1; Revelation 20:6) Thus, immortality involves eternal life but also deathlessness, unable to die, cannot be destroyed, while eternal life here on earth does not involve these things.

CHAPTER 17 What Does the Bible Really Say About the Resurrection?

All of us have lost a loved one to this force to be reckoned with, and it is only a matter of time before we have to face the greatest enemy humankind has ever known, death! However, we have been given a hope that is as great as the penalty that we are under. We have the hope of life eternal, and if we die, it is the hope of a resurrection. This hope means we will be reunited with the loved ones we lost. Some in the past have had a foretaste of this great hope:

Mark 5:35, 41-42 Updated American Standard Version (UASV)

35 While he was still speaking, they came from the house of the synagogue official, saying, "Your daughter has died; why trouble the Teacher anymore?" 41 Taking the child by the hand, he said to her, "Talitha koum!" (which is translated, "Little girl, I say to you, get up!"). 42 And immediately the girl got up and began walking (for she was twelve years old), and immediately they were amazed and completely astounded.

Acts 9:36-41 Updated American Standard Version (UASV)

36 Now in Joppa there was a disciple named Tabitha (which translated in Greek is called Dorcas); this woman was full of good deeds of kindness and good works which she continually did. 37 Now it happened that in those days she became ill and died, and when they had washed her, they laid her in an upper room. 38 Since Lydda was near Joppa, the disciples, having heard that Peter was there, sent two men to him, imploring him, "Do not delay in coming to us." 39 So Peter arose and went with them. When he arrived, they brought him into the upper room; and all the widows stood beside him, weeping and showing all the tunics and garments that Dorcas used to make while she was with them. 40 But Peter put them all

outside and knelt down and prayed; and turning to the body he said, "Tabitha, arise." And she opened her eyes, and when she saw Peter, she sat up. ⁴¹ And he gave her his hand and raised her up. Then, calling the holy ones and widows, he presented her alive.

We have already heard of the charges that Satan has risen against God in chapter six of this book. The resurrection hope allows God to let Satan play out his challenges to resolve the issues that would have otherwise plagued us for an eternity. It is like when you suffer through a painful medical treatment, to enjoy thereafter with all the complications of the issues you had. It is only by means of the greatest resurrection, namely Jesus Christ, that we can have this hope.

Matthew 20:28 Updated American Standard Version (UASV)
²⁸ even as the Son of Man came not to be served but to serve, and to give his soul as a ransom for many."

Resurrection is a Foundational Doctrine

Hebrews 6:1-2 Updated American Standard Version (UASV)

¹ Therefore, leaving behind the elementary doctrine about the Christ, let us press on to maturity, not laying again a foundation of repentance from dead works and faith in God, ² and of instruction about washings, the laying on of hands, the resurrection of the dead, and eternal judgment.

The resurrection is a foundational doctrine of our Christian faith. However, it does not fit into the world of humankind that is alienated from God. They see this as the only life there is, and so they are in pursuit of fleshly pleasures to make the most of it. The mindset of some of the first century was, "If the dead are not raised, 'Let us eat and drink, for tomorrow we die.'" (1 Cor. 15:32) On the other hand, we do not need to chase after the things that Satan's world has to offer.

Acts 17:32 Updated American Standard Version (UASV)
³² Now when they heard of the resurrection of the dead, some

mocked, but others said, "We will hear you concerning this also again."

We need to look at two **hopes** humans have the opportunity to have. Some are of new Israel and are seen as being given a kingdom, a chosen race, a royal priesthood, and ruling with Christ for a thousand years. There will be a need to investigate this, and this section will be a little more complex than any other part of this book. It is crucial to all of us, so bear with me. I am going to quote some leading evangelical scholars at length.

<u>Revelation 5:9-10</u> Updated American Standard Version (UASV)
⁹ And they **sang a new song**, saying,

"Worthy are you to take the scroll and to open its seals, for you were slain, and purchased for God with your blood men from every tribe and language and people and nation, ¹⁰ and you have made them **a kingdom and priests** to our God, and they **shall reign over the earth**."

> A further result of the Lamb's sacrifice is the establishment[2] of the redeemed as a kingdom and priests: *kai epoiēsas autous tō theō hēmōn basileian kai hiereis* ("and You made them a kingdom and priests to our God"). The threefold occurrence of this theme in Revelation (cf. also Rev. 1:6; 20:6) indicates that talk about such a spiritual heritage was common parlance among Christians of John's day (Swete). As God's possession,[3] the redeemed will not merely be God's people over whom He reigns, but will also share God's rule in the coming millennial kingdom (cf. 1 Cor. 4:8; 6:3) (Charles; Ladd). This kingdom is the goal toward which the program of God is moving as emphasized

---

[2] The aorist ἐποίησας connotes finished result. As commonly the case in the heavenly songs of this book, it is proleptic, anticipating the culmination of the process being carried out at the time the song is sung (Swete, *Apocalypse*, p. 81; Beckwith, *Apocalypse*, pp. 512–13).

[3] Τῷ θεῷ (5:10) has a possessive sense: "belonging to God" as His peculiar people (Beckwith, *Apocalypse*, p. 513).

by *basileusousin* ("they shall reign") later in v. 10 (cf. Rev. 20:4). The idea of priesthood found in *hiereis* ("priests") means full and immediate access into God's presence for the purpose of praise and worship (Ladd). It also includes the thought of priestly service to God (Mounce). Though believers are currently viewed as a royal priesthood (1 Pet. 2:5, 9; cf. Ex. 19:6), this is only preliminary to the fullness of the way they will function alongside Christ in the millennial kingdom.[4]

Kai basileusousin epi tēs gēs ("and they shall reign on the earth") explains more fully the earlier *basileian* ("kingdom"). The fact that believers will serve as reigning powers means that they will be the equivalent of kings (Charles; Beckwith). Spelled out more particularly in 20:4 regarding the millennial kingdom and in 22:5 regarding the eternal state, they will join with Christ in His continual reign following His second advent to the earth. This all stems from the epoch determining redemptive work of the Lamb.[5]

Revelation 5:9-10 has a high level of theological content. It either says that Jesus and his co-rulers will rule from heaven, over the earth, or on the earth. It is theological bias to have several cases of similar context and the same grammatical construction, rendering the verses the same every time, yet to then render one verse contrary to the others simply because it aligns with one's theology. Whether that is the case here or not, the readers must determine for themselves. The point, regardless, is this, either way, Jesus is ruling the earth, and we are blessed to have had his ransom sacrifice and resurrection. Slow down for the next few pages, as things will get a little deeper. We can grasp it if we just slow down, meditate on what is being said, get out our dictionary if we have to, and write the definitions in the book beside the word, and read again.

---

[4] Newell, Revelation, p. 13.

[5] Robert L. Thomas, Revelation 1-7: An Exegetical Commentary (Chicago: Moody Publishers, 1992), 402.

WHAT WILL HAPPEN If YOU DIE?

Heavenly Hope

Revelation 14:1-4 Updated American Standard Version (UASV)

14 Then I looked, and behold, the Lamb was standing on Mount Zion, and with him **one hundred and forty-four thousand**, having his name and the name of his Father written on their foreheads. ² And I heard a voice from heaven, like the sound of many waters and like the sound of loud thunder, and the voice which I heard was like the sound of harpists playing on their harps. ³ And **they sang a new song**[6] before the throne and before the four living creatures and the elders; and **no one could learn the song except the one hundred and forty-four thousand who had been purchased from the earth**. ⁴ These are the ones who have not been defiled with women, for they are virgins. These are the ones who follow the Lamb wherever He goes. These have been purchased from among men as first fruits to God and to the Lamb.

The whole of chapter 14 is proleptic. As a summary of the Millennium (20:4–6), the first five verses feature the Lamb in place of the beast, the Lamb's followers with His and the Father's seal in place of the beast's followers with the mark of the beast, and the divinely controlled Mount Zion in place of the pagan-controlled earth (Alford, Moffatt, Kiddle).[7]

Revelation 7:4 Updated American Standard Version (UASV)

⁴ And I heard the number of the ones who were sealed, one hundred forty-four thousand sealed from every tribe of the sons of Israel:

> Various efforts have sought to determine the significance of the number 144,000. An understanding of

---

[6] TR WH NU have ᾄδουσιν [ὡς] ᾠδὴν καινήν
("they sing, as it were, a new song"), which is supported by A C 051 Maj^a. However, all modern-day English versions have the variant reading αδουσιν ωδην καινην ("they sing a new song"), which is supported by P^{47} P^{115vid} ℵ P 046 2053 2344.

[7] Robert L. Thomas, Revelation 8-22: An Exegetical Commentary (Chicago: Moody Publishers, 1995), 189.

the number as symbolical divides it into three of its multiplicands, 12 × 12 × 1000. From the symbolism of the three it is concluded that the number indicates fixedness and fullest completeness.[8] Twelve, a number of the tribes, is both squared and multiplied by a thousand. This is a twofold way of emphasizing completeness (Mounce). It thus affirms the full number of God's people to be brought through tribulation (Ladd). The symbolic approach points out the impossibility of taking the number literally. It is simply a vast number, less than a number indefinitely great (cf. 7:9), but greater than a large number designedly finite (e.g., 1,000, Rev. 20:2) (Lee). Other occurrences of the numerical components that are supposedly symbolic are also pointed out, 12 thousand in Rev. 21:16, 12 in Rev. 22:2, and 24, a multiple of 12, in Rev. 4:4. This is done to enhance the case for symbolism (Johnson). Though admittedly ingenious, the case for symbolism is exegetically weak. The principal reason for the view is a predisposition to make the 144,000 into a group representative of the church with which no possible numerical connection exists. No justification can be found for understanding the simple statement of fact in v. 4 as a figure of speech. It is a definite number in contrast with the indefinite number of 7:9. If it is taken symbolically, no number in the book can be taken literally. As God reserved 7,000 in the days of Ahab (1 Kings 19:18; Rom. 11:4), He will reserve 144,000 for Himself during the future Great Tribulation.[9] (Thomas, Revelation 1-7: An Exegetical Commentary 1992, 473-74)

---

[8] Alford, Greek Testament, 4:624; Charles, Revelation, 1:206; Lenski, Revelation, p. 154.

[9] Bullinger, Apocalypse, p. 282. Geyser is correct in observing that the predominant concern of the Apocalypse is "the restoration [on earth] of the twelve tribes of Israel, their restoration as a twelve-tribe kingdom, in a renewed and purified city of David, under the rule of the victorious 'Lion of the Tribe of Judah, the Root of David' (5:5; 22:16)" (Albert Geyser, "The Twelve Tribes in Revelation: Judean and Judeo Christian Apocalypticism," NTS 23, no. 3 [July 1982]: 389). He is wrong,

These ones are made up of those under the new covenant, the Law of Christ, those **called out of natural Israel**, and the new Israelites, also known as the Israel of God. They are a chosen number that is to reign with Jesus as kings, priests, and judges. Therefore, we ask, what is the other hope?

The New Earth: The Earthly Hope

In the O[ld] T[estament] the kingdom of God is usually described in terms of a redeemed earth; this is especially clear in the book of Isaiah, where the final state of the universe is already called new heavens and a new earth (65:17; 66:22) The nature of this renewal was perceived only very dimly by OT authors, but they did express the belief that a humans ultimate destiny is an earthly one.[10] This vision is clarified in the N[ew] T[estament]. Jesus speaks of the "renewal" of the world (Matt 19:28), Peter of the restoration of all things (Acts 3:21). Paul writes that the universe will be redeemed by God from its current state of bondage (Rom. 8:18-21). This is confirmed by Peter, who describes the new heavens and the new earth as the Christian's hope (2 Pet. 3:13). Finally, the book of Revelation includes a glorious vision of the end of the present universe and the creation of a new universe, full of righteousness and the presence of God. The vision is confirmed by God in the awesome declaration: "I am making everything new!" (Rev. 21:1-8)

The new heavens and the new earth will be the renewed creation that will fulfill the purpose for which God created the universe. It will be characterized by the complete rule of God and by the full realization of the final goal of redemption: "Now the dwelling of God is with men" (Rev. 21:3).

---

however, in his theory that this belief characterized the Judean church only and was not shared by Gentile Christianity spearheaded by Paul (ibid., p. 390).

[10] It is unwise to speak of the written Word of God as if it were of human origin, saying, 'OT authors express the belief,' when what was written is the meaning and message of what God wanted to convey by means of the human author.

The fact that the universe will be created anew[11] shows that God's goals for humans is not an ethereal and disembodied existence but a bodily existence on a perfected earth. The scene of the beatific vision is the new earth. The spiritual does not exclude the created order and will be fully realized only within a perfected creation. (Elwell 2001, 828-29)

What have we learned so far in this blog? God created the earth to be inhabited, to be filled with perfect humans, who are over the animals, and under the sovereignty of God. (Gen 1:28; 2:8, 15; Ps 104:5; 115:16; Eccl 1:4) Sin did not dissuade God from his plans (Isa. 45:18); hence, he has saved redeemable humankind by Jesus' ransom sacrifice. It seems that the Bible offers two hopes to redeemed humans, **(1) a heavenly hope**, or **(2) an earthly hope**. It also seems that those with heavenly hope are limited in number and are going to heaven to rule with Christ as kings, priests, and judges either **on** the earth or **over** the earth from heaven. It seems that those with earthly hope will receive eternal life here on a paradise earth as originally intended.

---

[11] Creating anew does not mean complete destruction followed by a re-creation, but instead a renewal of the present universe.

CHAPTER 18 Does the Concept of Hell Align with Biblical Teachings of Justice and Love?

The concept of hell, especially as a place of eternal torment, has been a subject of intense debate and interpretation within Christian theology. This chapter critically examines this concept, considering the original biblical languages, contextual interpretations, and the nature of God as depicted in the scriptures. It seeks to answer whether the traditional understanding of hell aligns with the Biblical portrayal of God's justice and love.

Understanding Sheol, Hades, and Gehenna

1. **Sheol and Hades**: In the Old Testament, "Sheol" (שאול) is a term used to describe the abode of the dead, a place of darkness where both the righteous and unrighteous go (Ecclesiastes 9:10; Genesis 42:38). The Greek equivalent in the New Testament is "Hades" (Ἅδης). These terms reflect a state of death rather than a place of fiery torment.

2. **Gehenna**: In contrast, "Gehenna" (γέεννα) in the New Testament, which Jesus mentions, refers to the Valley of Hinnom near Jerusalem, historically a site of child sacrifices (Jeremiah 7:31). Jesus used Gehenna metaphorically to symbolize final destruction, not endless suffering (Mark 9:43-48).

Biblical Depictions of Final Judgment

1. **Symbolic Language**: Jesus often used parables and symbolic language to convey spiritual truths. The descriptions of fire in Gehenna are symbolic of complete destruction, not eternal suffering (Matthew 13:42; Mark 9:43-48).

2. **Annihilation vs Eternal Torment**: The concept of annihilation, which is the complete and final destruction of the wicked, is more consistent with the Biblical narrative than eternal torment. This is evident in the imagery used in Revelation where death and Hades are thrown into the lake of fire, symbolizing their ultimate end (Revelation 20:14, 21:8).

The Character of God and the Concept of Hell

1. **God's Justice**: The doctrine of eternal torment in hell seems inconsistent with Biblical teachings on justice. Romans 6:23 states that the wages of sin is death, not eternal torment. This suggests a finality in death that is inconsistent with the concept of unending suffering.

2. **God's Love**: The essence of God's character, as revealed in the Bible, is love (1 John 4:8). The idea of a loving God inflicting eternal pain is contradictory to this character. It is more consistent to interpret God's judgment as ultimately just and merciful, leading to either restoration or final destruction.

The Parable of the Rich Man and Lazarus

1. **Interpreting Parables**: The story of the rich man and Lazarus (Luke 16:19-31) is a parable, not a literal depiction of the afterlife. It was used to teach about social injustices and the reversal of fortunes in God's kingdom, rather than to provide a detailed account of hell.

Reexamining Hell in Light of Scripture

1. **Scriptural Consistency**: A thorough examination of the scriptures in their original languages and contexts reveals that the traditional concept of hell as a place of eternal torment is not consistent with the overarching themes of love, justice, and finality of judgment presented in the Bible.

2. **Theological Implications**: This understanding impacts how Christians view God, justice, and the afterlife. It encourages a relationship with God based on love and respect rather than fear of eternal torment.

In conclusion, the Biblical evidence, when examined in its original languages and contexts, does not support the traditional view of hell as a place of eternal fiery torment. Rather, it portrays a God of justice and love, whose final judgment leads to either restoration or complete destruction. This interpretation aligns more closely with the scriptural depiction of God's character and the overall narrative of redemption and justice in the Bible.

Edward D. Andrews

CHAPTER 19 What Has Happened to Hellfire: Revisiting the Doctrine Through a Biblical Lens

The concept of hell has been a central yet controversial topic in Christian theology. This chapter aims to explore the evolution of the doctrine of hellfire, examining scriptural evidence, historical interpretations, and the theological implications of various beliefs about hell.

Scriptural Foundations of Hell

1. **Old Testament Perspectives**: In the Hebrew Bible, the concept of Sheol (שאול) is prevalent. Sheol is often translated as "grave" or "pit" and is depicted as a place of darkness to which all the dead go, irrespective of their moral choices in life (Ecclesiastes 9:10, Genesis 42:38).

2. **New Testament Developments**: The New Testament introduces terms like Hades (Ἅδης) and Gehenna (γέεννα). Hades corresponds to Sheol, while Gehenna, referring to the Valley of Hinnom, becomes a metaphor for final judgment and destruction, not eternal torment (Mark 9:43-48).

Historical Evolution of the Concept of Hell

1. **Early Christian Views**: The early Church Fathers had varied interpretations of hell. While Justin Martyr and Tertullian saw it as a place of fire and torment, Origen and

Gregory of Nyssa viewed it more as a state of separation from God.

2. **Medieval and Reformation Era**: Augustine's view of hell as both a place of physical and spiritual suffering gained prominence in the medieval church. During the Reformation, figures like Luther and Calvin saw hell's fiery torment as figurative of separation from God.

3. **Modern Interpretations**: The 20th century saw a significant shift, with many theologians and denominations viewing hell more as a metaphorical state of separation from God or non-existence, rather than a place of eternal fiery torment.

Biblical Analysis of Hellfire

1. **Literal vs. Symbolic Interpretation**: The imagery of fire in scriptures is often symbolic, representing purification, judgment, or destruction. The depiction of hell as a fiery place in some New Testament passages should be understood metaphorically, in line with the Jewish use of Gehenna as a symbol of divine judgment.

2. **Justice and Mercy of God**: The doctrine of eternal torment in a fiery hell seems inconsistent with the Biblical portrayal of God's nature as just and merciful. Scriptures emphasize God's desire for repentance and restoration rather than eternal punishment (Ezekiel 18:23).

3. **Annihilationism**: This perspective, which views the wicked as being ultimately destroyed or ceasing to exist, aligns more with scriptures that speak of the finality and completeness of God's judgment (2 Thessalonians 1:9).

Theological Implications

1. **God's Character**: Understanding hell in terms of separation or annihilation rather than eternal torment aligns

more closely with the Biblical depiction of God as loving, just, and merciful.

2. **Human Destiny and Free Will:** This interpretation respects human free will and the ultimate consequences of choices made in life, emphasizing the finality of God's judgment in a way that aligns with His character.

The traditional concept of hell as a place of eternal fiery torment has evolved over time and is subject to various interpretations. A thorough examination of the Biblical texts suggests that hell is more accurately understood as a state of separation from God or as complete destruction, rather than as a place of unending physical torment. This understanding is more consistent with the overarching themes of God's justice, mercy, and love in the Bible.

CHAPTER 20 What Really Is Hell? Reevaluating the Doctrine in Light of Scripture

The concept of hell has been a subject of deep theological reflection and debate throughout the history of Christian thought. This chapter seeks to explore the Biblical understanding of hell, examining scriptural evidence and theological interpretations to determine its true nature.

The Nature of Death According to the Bible

1. **Death as a Consequence of Sin**: Romans 5:12 and 6:23 articulate that sin brought death into the world, and death is the wages of sin. This establishes death, not torment after death, as the primary consequence of sin.

2. **The State of the Dead**: Scriptural texts such as Ecclesiastes 9:5, 10, and Psalm 146:4 indicate that the dead are in a state of non-existence, devoid of consciousness or activity. This challenges the notion of the dead experiencing suffering or pleasure.

Understanding the Biblical Concept of the Soul

1. **The Soul in Genesis**: Genesis 2:7 describes Adam as becoming a "living soul" (נפש חיה), emphasizing that the soul is not an immortal entity within a person, but the person as a whole.

2. **Mortality of the Soul**: Ezekiel 18:4 clearly states that the soul can die, contradicting the idea of an inherently immortal soul that lives on post-mortem in a place like hell.

Hell in Biblical Language

1. **Sheol and Hades**: The Hebrew word Sheol (שאול) and its Greek equivalent Hades (Ἅδης) refer to the common grave of mankind, not a place of fiery torment. This is evidenced by their usage in contexts describing the abode of the dead in general (Acts 2:31; Job 14:13).

2. **Gehenna – Symbol of Destruction**: Gehenna (γέεννα) in the New Testament, used by Jesus in Matthew 5:22 and Mark 9:47, 48, symbolizes complete destruction or annihilation, rather than eternal suffering. It draws on the imagery of the Valley of Hinnom, a place of refuse burning outside Jerusalem.

The Symbolism of Fire in Biblical Teachings

1. **Fire as a Symbol of Destruction**: Fire in Biblical literature often symbolizes destruction and not torture. Revelation 20:14 describes death and Hades being thrown into the "lake of fire," indicating the annihilation of death and the grave.

2. **Annihilation vs Eternal Torment**: This use of fire imagery aligns more closely with the concept of annihilation, the permanent end of existence, as opposed to ongoing torment.

Resurrection and Hell

1. **Jesus' Death and Resurrection**: Jesus' own experience, as recounted in Acts 2:31 and 1 Corinthians 15:3, 4, where he was in Hades (the grave) and then resurrected, underscores

the understanding of hell as the grave rather than a place of eternal torment.

2. **Hope for the Dead**: Revelation 20:13 and John 5:28, 29 offer a perspective of hope, indicating a future resurrection for those in the grave, contrary to the idea of irrevocable suffering in hell.

The Biblical evidence, when examined in its original languages and contexts, indicates that hell is not a place of eternal fiery torment. Instead, hell (Sheol/Hades) is better understood as the common grave of mankind, with death being a state of nonexistence. Gehenna represents complete destruction or annihilation. This understanding is more consistent with the Biblical themes of God's justice, mercy, and the hope of resurrection, affirming that death, not eternal torment, is the consequence of sin. This reevaluation offers a more compassionate and just view of the divine nature and the ultimate destiny of humanity.

Edward D. Andrews

CHAPTER 21 Hellfire—Flaring or Fading? A Historical and Theological Inquiry

The concept of hellfire, once a cornerstone in Christian doctrine, has undergone significant shifts in perception and interpretation. This chapter delves into the historical evolution of the doctrine, its Biblical basis, and the reasons behind its fluctuating prominence in Christian thought.

Historical Perspective on the Doctrine of Hell

1. **The Era of Fire and Brimstone**: In the 18th century, as epitomized by Jonathan Edwards' sermons, the imagery of hell as a place of eternal, fiery torment was vivid and terrifying, serving as a moral deterrent.

2. **The Decline of Hellfire**: The 19th and 20th centuries witnessed a gradual fading of this stark depiction. Factors such as modern intellectualism and the horrors of world events like Hiroshima and the Holocaust contributed to a reevaluation of the traditional views of hell.

3. **Hell's Resurgence in Modern Times**: Despite its decline in some theological circles, the concept of hell has seen a resurgence in recent years, especially within evangelical movements. This revival raises questions about hell's nature and relevance in contemporary Christianity.

Biblical Foundations of Hell

1. **Sheol and Hades**: In the Bible, Sheol (שאול) in Hebrew and Hades (Ἅδης) in Greek refer to the grave or the abode of

the dead, not necessarily a place of torment (Ecclesiastes 9:10, Acts 2:31).

2. **Gehenna – A Symbol of Destruction**: Gehenna (γέεννα) is used in the New Testament as a metaphor for final judgment and destruction, drawing from the imagery of the Valley of Hinnom, a waste disposal site outside Jerusalem (Matthew 5:22, Mark 9:47).

3. **Symbolism of Fire**: Biblically, fire often symbolizes purification or destruction rather than eternal torment. The "lake of fire" in Revelation symbolizes complete annihilation rather than unending suffering (Revelation 20:14).

Theological and Philosophical Considerations

1. **Reconciling Hell with Divine Attributes**: The traditional view of hell as a place of endless torment raises questions about its compatibility with the attributes of a loving and just God.

2. **Annihilationism vs. Eternal Torment**: Some Christian scholars advocate annihilationism—the belief that the wicked cease to exist rather than suffer eternally—as a more consistent interpretation with the Biblical narrative.

3. **Universalism and Conditional Immortality**: Alternative views like Universalism (all will eventually be saved) and Conditional Immortality (only the saved receive eternal life) have also gained traction in modern theological discussions.

Impact on Christian Life and Thought

1. **The Role of Hell in Christian Morality**: The doctrine of hell has historically played a role in shaping moral behavior and the fear of divine judgment. Its fluctuating emphasis

reflects changing attitudes toward sin, salvation, and divine justice.

2. **Theological Diversity Within Christianity**: The varied interpretations of hell underscore the diversity within Christian theology and the ongoing struggle to understand and articulate the complexities of the afterlife.

The concept of hellfire has evolved significantly throughout Christian history. While its portrayal as a place of eternal torment has been dominant in certain periods, modern theological thought has seen a shift towards more nuanced interpretations. These include views of hell as a state of annihilation, a metaphor for separation from God, or a condition of non-existence. This reevaluation reflects a broader theological endeavor to reconcile the doctrine of hell with the Biblical narrative and the character of God as revealed in Scripture. The ongoing debate and study of hell demonstrate the dynamic nature of Christian theology and its response to changing cultural and intellectual contexts.

CHAPTER 22 Eternal Torment—Why a Disturbing Doctrine? An In-Depth Examination

The doctrine of eternal torment in hell has been a fundamental yet highly contentious belief in Christianity. Its moral implications and theological soundness have been subjects of intense debate. This chapter seeks to explore the origins, development, and challenges of this doctrine, critically examining it in light of scriptural evidence and theological reasoning.

The Historical Development of the Doctrine of Eternal Torment

1. **Early Christianity and Hell**: The concept of eternal punishment in hell is not prominently featured in early Christian writings. It gained more prominence in the Middle Ages, influenced by works like Dante's "Inferno."

2. **Jonathan Edwards and the Revival of Hellfire**: In the 18th century, preachers like Jonathan Edwards vividly described hell as a place of fire and brimstone, reinforcing the doctrine of eternal torment in the collective consciousness of believers.

3. **The Fading and Resurgence of the Doctrine**: Over the centuries, the emphasis on eternal torment has fluctuated, with periods of decline and resurgence influenced by cultural, theological, and historical factors.

Scriptural Analysis of Hell and Eternal Punishment

1. **New Testament References**: Key passages often cited in support of eternal torment include references to Gehenna (γέεννα) and the "lake of fire" in Revelation. These need to be interpreted in their historical and cultural contexts.

2. **The Parables of Jesus**: Jesus' use of parables about judgment and punishment (e.g., the Rich Man and Lazarus) must be understood metaphorically rather than as literal descriptions of the afterlife.

3. **The Hebrew Concept of Sheol**: In the Old Testament, Sheol (שאול) refers to a general state of the dead, without implying eternal conscious torment.

Moral and Theological Challenges

1. **Divine Justice and Love**: The idea of eternal torment seems to conflict with the Biblical portrayal of God as loving, merciful, and just. Endless punishment appears disproportionate to the finite sins of human beings.

2. **The Problem of Suffering**: Eternal torment raises significant moral dilemmas about the nature of suffering and divine justice. It challenges the notion of a compassionate and forgiving God.

3. **Influence on Human Behavior**: The belief in a God who inflicts eternal torment can have profound implications on moral and ethical behavior, potentially encouraging a punitive rather than a rehabilitative view of justice.

Alternative Theological Views

1. **Annihilationism**: This view posits that the wicked will ultimately be destroyed and cease to exist rather than suffer eternally.

2. **Universal Reconciliation**: Some theologians propose that all souls will eventually be reconciled to God, emphasizing God's overarching love and mercy.

3. **Conditional Immortality**: This perspective holds that eternal life is a gift granted only to the righteous, while the unrighteous face permanent death, not eternal torment.

Evaluating Biblical Fidelity and Doctrine

1. **Scriptural Interpretation**: A critical examination of the Biblical texts suggests that the traditional doctrine of eternal torment may be more a product of historical theology than of clear scriptural mandate.

2. **The Role of Context and Hermeneutics**: Understanding the historical and cultural contexts of Biblical texts is crucial in interpreting passages related to hell and judgment.

The doctrine of eternal torment poses significant moral and theological challenges. It conflicts with modern sensibilities of justice and the Biblical portrayal of God's character. An honest and thorough examination of the scriptural texts, along with a consideration of historical and cultural contexts, suggests that this doctrine may need reevaluation. Alternative interpretations like annihilationism, universal reconciliation, and conditional immortality offer more coherent and compassionate understandings of the fate of the wicked in the afterlife, aligning more closely with the overarching themes of love, justice, and mercy in the Bible.

… Edward D. Andrews

CHAPTER 23 Hell—Eternal Torture or Common Grave? Reexamining the Doctrine in Light of Scripture

The doctrine of hell has long been a subject of theological debate within Christianity. Traditionally portrayed as a place of eternal torment, this view has been increasingly challenged by scholars who argue for a more nuanced understanding based on scriptural analysis. This chapter aims to explore these perspectives and examine what the Bible truly says about hell.

Historical Perspectives on Hell

1. **Early Christian Views**: The early Church Fathers and medieval theologians often depicted hell as a place of everlasting torment, a view that was later reinforced during the Reformation.

2. **Changing Perceptions**: In recent times, theologians like John R. W. Stott have challenged the traditional view, arguing for annihilationism based on scriptural evidence, suggesting that the wicked will ultimately face destruction rather than eternal suffering.

The Biblical Language of Destruction

1. **Greek Terminology**: Key to understanding the doctrine of hell is the Greek language of the New Testament. Terms like "apollumi" (to destroy) and "apòleia" (destruction) are often used in contexts related to final judgment and hell (Gehenna).

2. **Scriptural Usage**: These terms, as used in the Bible, often denote an end or cessation of existence rather than ongoing torment. For example, Matthew 10:28 speaks of God destroying both soul and body in hell, implying cessation rather than eternal suffering.

Interpreting the Imagery of Fire

1. **Symbolism in Biblical Texts**: The imagery of fire in the Bible, while evocative of pain, is more frequently used to symbolize complete destruction. This can be seen in the use of Gehenna, which historically referred to a physical location outside Jerusalem where waste was burned.
2. **New Testament Descriptions**: Passages like Mark 9:47-48 and Revelation 14:9-11 that describe fire and torment are often symbolic, reflecting the destruction of the wicked rather than their eternal conscious torment.

Theological Implications of Annihilationism

1. **Rethinking Eternal Punishment**: Annihilationism posits that the wicked will ultimately cease to exist, which aligns more closely with the Biblical portrayal of God as just and merciful.
2. **Moral and Ethical Considerations**: The traditional doctrine of eternal torment raises significant moral dilemmas about God's nature and justice, which are addressed more coherently by the annihilationist perspective.

Reconciling Hell with God's Justice

1. **Divine Justice and Mercy**: The concept of a loving and just God seems at odds with the idea of eternal torment. Annihilationism presents a view of divine justice that is

more consistent with God's character as revealed in the Bible.

2. **Proportionality of Punishment**: The annihilationist view also addresses the concern about the disproportionality of eternal torment for finite human sins, aligning with Biblical principles of justice.

Examining Key Theological Concepts

1. **The Immortality of the Soul**: Traditional views of hell are often tied to the belief in the innate immortality of the soul. However, a closer examination of the Biblical texts suggests that this concept is not explicitly supported by scripture.

2. **The Resurrection and Judgment**: The Bible teaches that the dead will be resurrected for judgment. This aligns more with the idea of a final judgment leading to either life or cessation of existence, rather than unending torment.

The doctrine of hell as eternal torment is increasingly being reevaluated in light of scriptural evidence. The Biblical language of destruction, the symbolism of fire, and the theological implications of a just and merciful God point towards an understanding of hell as a state of annihilation rather than perpetual suffering. This perspective not only aligns more closely with the scriptural text but also offers a more coherent and ethically sound portrayal of divine justice.

CHAPTER 24 What Did Jesus Teach About Hell? Analyzing Scriptural References and Interpretations

The doctrine of hell, particularly the concept of eternal torment, has been a contentious topic in Christian theology. Central to this debate are the teachings of Jesus Christ, who spoke about hell in various contexts. This chapter seeks to examine Jesus' teachings on hell, considering their historical and cultural context and their implications for understanding the nature of hell.

Jesus' References to Hell in the Gospels

1. **Gehenna - The Valley of Hinnom**: Jesus' use of the term Gehenna (Greek: Γέεννα) refers to the Valley of Hinnom, a location outside Jerusalem historically associated with pagan sacrifices and later used as a garbage dump where fires continually burned. Jesus used Gehenna symbolically to represent the final judgment and destruction, not a place of eternal torment (Mark 9:47-48).

2. **The Symbolism of Fire and Worms**: In Mark 9:48, Jesus alludes to Isaiah 66:24, using the imagery of undying worms and unquenchable fire. This reference, in its original context, speaks to the disgrace of unburied corpses rather than the torment of living souls, suggesting a metaphor for complete destruction or disgrace in death rather than ongoing suffering.

Interpretation of Eternal Fire and Punishment

1. **Matthew 25:41, 46 - Eternal Fire and Punishment**: In these verses, Jesus speaks of "eternal fire" and "eternal punishment." However, considering the symbolic language used elsewhere in Scripture, these terms likely symbolize a final and irreversible judgment, rather than perpetual conscious torment.

2. **The Nature of Eternal Punishment**: The Greek word for punishment used here, "kolasis," originally meant pruning or cutting off, implying not ongoing torment but a permanent cessation of life or existence, a complete cutting off from God and His blessings.

Jesus' Teachings in Context

1. **Cultural and Historical Background**: Understanding Jesus' teachings on hell requires consideration of the first-century Jewish context. Jewish views on the afterlife in Jesus' time were diverse and did not uniformly include the concept of eternal torment in a fiery hell.

2. **Jesus' Use of Parables and Symbolism**: Jesus often used parables and symbolic language to convey deeper spiritual truths. His references to hell should be interpreted within this framework, as metaphoric teachings on divine judgment and the consequences of sin.

Jesus' Emphasis on Resurrection and Life

1. **Resurrection as Central to Jesus' Teachings**: Jesus' teachings focused more on the resurrection and the promise of eternal life for the righteous (John 5:25-29; 11:25). The concept of resurrection contradicts the notion of the soul's

inherent immortality and ongoing existence in a place like hell.

2. **The Message of Hope and Redemption**: Jesus' teachings consistently emphasized God's desire for repentance and redemption rather than the eternal punishment of the wicked (John 3:16).

Theological Implications of Jesus' Teachings on Hell

1. **Reconciling Hell with God's Nature**: The interpretation of hell as eternal torment poses challenges when reconciling it with the Biblical portrayal of God as loving, merciful, and just. Jesus' teachings, when understood in their historical and cultural context, present a more coherent picture of divine judgment.

2. **The Role of Hell in Christian Doctrine**: Understanding hell in the light of Jesus' teachings shifts the focus from eternal torment to the finality of God's judgment and the urgency of repentance and moral living.

Jesus' teachings about hell, when examined in their scriptural and historical context, do not support the traditional doctrine of hell as a place of eternal conscious torment. Instead, they point towards a symbolic representation of final judgment and the irreversible consequences of rejecting God's offer of salvation. This interpretation aligns more closely with the overarching themes of redemption, resurrection, and the loving and just nature of God as presented in the teachings of Jesus Christ.

Edward D. Andrews

CHAPTER 25 The Rich Man and Lazarus: What is the Underlying Message in Jesus' Parable?

The parable of the Rich Man and Lazarus, recounted by Jesus in Luke 16:19-31, has been subject to various interpretations throughout Christian history. This chapter seeks to explore the deeper meanings of this parable, considering its context, symbolism, and the teachings of Jesus about life, death, and the hereafter.

Contextual Background of the Parable

1. **Audience and Setting**: When Jesus narrated this parable, He was addressing the Pharisees, known for their love of money and self-righteousness. This audience is crucial for understanding the parable's intended message.

2. **Contrast with Preceding Teachings**: Jesus' preceding teachings emphasized the proper use of riches and the inability to serve both God and wealth. This parable further illustrates the spiritual dangers of misusing wealth and ignoring spiritual needs.

Symbolic Representation in the Parable

1. **The Rich Man**: Symbolically, the rich man represents the Jewish religious leaders, particularly the Pharisees. His luxurious life and neglect of Lazarus mirror their spiritual

pride, material wealth, and indifference to the needs of the common people.

2. **Lazarus**: Lazarus, a beggar covered in sores, symbolizes the marginalized and spiritually needy individuals who were often overlooked or scorned by the religious elite.

3. **The Deaths and Their Aftermath**: The deaths of these two characters symbolize a significant shift. For the religious leaders (the rich man), it represents a fall from their privileged spiritual status. For the humble and ignored (Lazarus), it signifies elevation to a place of comfort and favor with God.

Interpretation of Key Elements

1. **Hades and Abraham's Bosom**: In the parable, Hades, where the rich man finds himself, is not portrayed as a fiery hell but as a place of anguish due to separation from God. Abraham's bosom, where Lazarus is comforted, symbolizes a state of favor and salvation.

2. **The Unbridgeable Chasm**: The chasm between the rich man and Lazarus reflects the irreversible consequences of one's choices in life concerning faith and conduct.

3. **The Dialogue Between the Rich Man and Abraham**: This conversation underscores the theme of irreversible divine judgment and the sufficiency of Moses and the prophets (i.e., the Scriptures) for guidance and salvation.

The Parable's Teachings on Afterlife and Resurrection

1. **Afterlife Imagery**: While the parable uses imagery of the afterlife, it is primarily symbolic, meant to convey lessons about justice, compassion, and the consequences of ignoring God's word.

2. **Resurrection and Final Judgment:** The conclusion of the parable, emphasizing the importance of heeding Scripture and the foreshadowing of the resurrection, aligns with Jesus' teachings on the final judgment and the resurrection of the dead.

Theological Implications

1. **Warning against Materialism and Spiritual Apathy:** The parable serves as a warning against the dangers of materialism, self-righteousness, and neglect of spiritual duties.

2. **Divine Justice and Mercy:** It illustrates the principles of divine justice and mercy, showing that God's judgment is based on one's faith and actions rather than their social or religious status.

3. **The Role of Scripture and Revelation:** The parable underscores the sufficiency of Scripture for salvation and ethical living, rejecting the notion that extraordinary signs or wonders are necessary for belief and repentance.

The parable of the Rich Man and Lazarus, far from being a literal depiction of the afterlife, is a profound teaching tool used by Jesus to convey essential spiritual truths. It highlights the dangers of wealth and complacency, the necessity of compassion and humility, and the irrevocable nature of God's judgment. This parable encourages a life of faith, adherence to God's word, and a focus on spiritual rather than material riches.

WHAT WILL HAPPEN If YOU DIE?

CHAPTER 26 Did God Mislead Humanity in Eden? Unpacking the True Consequences of Sin

The declaration in Genesis 2:17, where God warns Adam against eating from the tree of knowledge, stating he would "surely die," has sparked theological debates about the nature of sin's consequences. This chapter delves into Biblical texts to understand whether God's statement implied physical death or concealed a harsher reality of eternal torment.

God's Warning in Genesis: The Immediate Consequences

1. **The Context of Genesis 2:17**: God's warning to Adam is direct and unequivocal. The Hebrew phrase מוֹת תָּמוּת (mot tamut), translated as "you shall surely die," implies a definitive end, a cessation of life.

2. **Understanding Death in Biblical Terms**: In the Hebrew Bible, death is often portrayed as the end of earthly life, a return to the dust from which humans were made (Genesis 3:19). This perspective aligns with the warning given to Adam.

The Serpent's Contradiction and the Nature of Deception

1. **The Serpent's Claim**: In Genesis 3:4, the serpent counters God's warning by claiming that Adam and Eve would not

die. This statement can be seen as the first Biblical instance of deceit, directly challenging God's truth.

2. **Deception through Half-Truths**: The serpent's deception lay in twisting the truth. While Adam and Eve did gain knowledge of good and evil, they also experienced spiritual separation from God and eventual physical death, confirming God's warning.

The Consistency of Scriptural Teachings on Sin and Death

1. **Ezekiel 18:4 and the Soul's Mortality**: Ezekiel reiterates the principle that the soul (נֶפֶשׁ, nephesh) that sins shall die. This aligns with the Genesis account, emphasizing death as the primary consequence of sin.

2. **Romans 6:23 - Wages of Sin**: The Apostle Paul's statement in Romans 6:23 echoes the Genesis account, identifying death as the 'wages' or direct outcome of sin.

3. **2 Thessalonians 1:9 and Eternal Destruction**: Paul's reference to "eternal destruction" in 2 Thessalonians 1:9 further reinforces the concept of an irrevocable end, rather than eternal conscious torment.

Reevaluating the Doctrine of Eternal Torment

1. **Absence of Eternal Torment in Genesis**: The Genesis narrative does not mention eternal torment as a consequence of sin. This absence raises questions about the traditional doctrine of hell as a place of eternal suffering.

2. **Justice and God's Nature**: The notion of eternal torment seems inconsistent with the Biblical portrayal of God's justice and mercy. The penalties described in Genesis and throughout the Old Testament align more with physical

death and separation from God rather than perpetual torment.

Theological Implications and Modern Understanding

1. **Reinterpreting Traditional Views**: A reexamination of the Genesis account, in light of the entire Biblical canon, suggests a need to reinterpret traditional doctrines about the afterlife and the consequences of sin.

2. **Death and Resurrection in Christian Theology**: Christian theology's focus on resurrection and eternal life through Christ offers an alternative perspective to eternal torment, emphasizing redemption and restoration over endless suffering.

The Biblical narrative, starting from Genesis, consistently presents death as the only consequence of sin. This understanding aligns with God's nature as just and merciful and challenges traditional interpretations of eternal torment. A comprehensive analysis of scriptural texts suggests that God's warning to Adam in Eden was neither misleading nor incomplete but was a straightforward declaration of the gravity of disobedience and its ultimate consequence: death, both physical and spiritual.

Bibliography

Anders, M., & McIntosh, D. (2009). *Holman Old Testament Commentary - Deuteronomy (pp. 359-360)*. . Nashville: B&H Publishing.

Andrews, E. D. (2017). *HUMAN IMPERFECTION: While We Were Sinners Christ Died For Us.* Cambridge, OH: Christian Ppublishing House.

Andrews, E. D. (2023). *BIBLICAL EXEGESIS: Biblical Criticism on Trial.* Cambridge, OH: Christian Publishing House.

Andrews, E. D. (2023). *CHRISTIAN APOLOGETICS: Answering the Tough Questions: Evidence and Reason in Defense of the Faith.* Cambridge, Ohio: Christian Publishing House.

Andrews, E. D. (2023). *THE EXPOSITORY DICTIONARY: A Companion Study Tool to the Updated American Standard Version.* Cambridge, OH: Christian Publishing House.

Andrews, E. D. (2023). *UNSHAKABLE BELIEFS: Strategies for Strengthening and Defending Your Faith.* Cambridge, OH: Christian Publishing House.

Brand, C., Draper, C., & Archie, E. (2003). *Holman Illustrated Bible Dictionary: Revised, Updated and Expanded.* Nashville, TN: Holman.

Bratcher, R. G., & Hatton, H. (1993). *A Handbook on the Revelation to John.* New York: United Bible Societies.

Bromiley, G. W., & Friedrich, G. (1964-). *Theological Dictionary of the New Testament, ed. Gerhard Kittel, vol. 4.* Grand Rapids, MI: Eerdmans.

Bullinger, E. W. (1898). *Figures of Speech Used in the Bible.* London; New York: E. & J. B. Young & Co.

Elwell, W. A. (2001). *Evangelical Dictionary of Theology (Second Edition).* Grand Rapids: Baker Academic.

Erickson, M. J. (1998). *Christian Theology.* Grand Rapids, MI: Baker Academic.

Gangel, K. O. (2000). *Holman New Testament Commentary, vol. 4, John* . Nashville, TN: Broadman & Holman Publishers.

Kittel, G., Friedrich, G., & Bromiley, G. W. (1995, c1985). *Theological Dictionary of the New Testament.* Grand Rapids: Eerdmans.

Knight, G. W. (1992). *The Pastoral Epistles: A Commentary on the Greek Text, New International Greek Testament Commentary.* Grand Rapids, MI; Carlisle, England: W.B. Eerdmans; Paternoster Press.

Lea, T. D. (1999). *Holman New Testament Commentary: Vol. 10, Hebrews, James.* Nashville, TN: Broadman & Holman Publishers.

McReynolds, P. R. (1999). *Word Study: Greek-English.* Carol Stream: Tyndale House Publishers.

Mounce, W. D. (2006). *Mounce's Complete Expository Dictionary of Old & New Testament Words.* Grand Rapids, MI: Zondervan.

Sprinkle, P. (. (2016). *Four Views on Hell: Second Edition.* Grand Rapids, MI: Zondervan.

Stein, R. H. (1994). *A Basic Guide to Interpreting the Bible: Playing by the Rules.* Grand Rapids: Baker Books.

Thomas, R. L. (1992). *Revelation 1-7: An Exegetical Commentary* . Chicago, IL: Moody Publishers.

Thomas, R. L. (1995). *Revelation 8-22: An Exegetical Commentary* . Chicago, IL: Moody Publishers.

Towns, E. L. (2006). *Concise Bible Dictrines: Clear, Simple, and Easy-to-Understand Explanations of Bible Doctrines.* Chattanooga: AMG Publishers.

Vine, W. E. (1996). *Vine's Expository Dictionary of Old and New Testament Words.* Nashville: Thomas Nelson.

Zodhiates, S. (2000, c1992, c1993). *The Complete Word Study Dictionary: New Testament.* Chattanooga: AMG Publishers.

Zuck, R. B. (1991). *Basic Bible Interpretation: A Prafctical Guide to Discovering Biblical Truth.* Colorado Springs: David C. Cook.

WHAT WILL HAPPEN If YOU DIE?

www.ingramcontent.com/pod-product-compliance
Lightning Source LLC
Chambersburg PA
CBHW070449050426
42451CB00015B/3411